DOPE THERAPY

A RADICAL GUIDE TO OWNING YOUR THERAPY JOURNEY

DOPE THERAPY

A RADICAL GUIDE TO OWNING YOUR THERAPY JOURNEY

SHANI TRAN, LPCC

Publisher Mike Sanders
Senior Editor Ann Barton
Art Director William Thomas
Senior Designer Jessica Lee
Compositor Ayanna Lacey
Proofreaders Lisa Starnes, Georgette Beatty
Indexer Celia McCoy

First American Edition, 2022
Published in the United States by DK Publishing
6081 E. 82nd Street, Indianapolis, IN 46250

Library of Congress Catalog Number: 2022931015
ISBN 978-0-7440-5493-4

DK books are available at special discounts when purchased
in bulk for sales promotions, premiums, fundraising,
or educational use. For details, contact:
SpecialSales@dk.com

Printed and bound in the United States

For the curious
www.dk.com

To my girls.
May you know that you are capable
of resilience in the face of pain.

To my social media supporters and clients.
This book was written with you in mind.

CONTENTS

INTRODUCTION

Welcome to this crazy-a$$ journey of therapy. It is one that has the potential to change your life. I know this as both a therapist and a client.

I'm Shani T., by the way. I am a Licensed Professional Clinical Counselor in the state of Minnesota. My journey as a therapist started in undergrad, when I was hired for my first job, helping children diagnosed with autism. If you are wondering why I wrote this book, it's to help people like you navigate therapy.

I know what it is like to have pain and suffering and to want another option. I wrote this book to be a tool used alongside your therapy journey. This book is meant to help you from start, when you are thinking about going to therapy, to finish, when therapy has ended.

My expertise is validated through my dope #af resume. I have worked in a jail, at a day-treatment facility with teens, as an in-home counselor with parents to keep their kids who are on probation out of trouble, and at a medical insurance company on the behavioral health team. I now own and operate a group private practice.

But that's not where my helping expertise ends. I also have a TikTok where I twerk, play characters, and empower people to own their mental health journey. Most of this book will be about helping you navigate the journey, so to kick it off, I thought we could start with talking about me and my own therapy journey.

WHAT IF I DON'T HEAL?

It had been roughly four years since I had thought about taking my life. I had just had my first child. My husband and I had moved to Minnesota while I was pregnant, so I hadn't made any friends yet. My only support system was him. After having my daughter, we realized we couldn't afford daycare and the best thing to do was for me to become a stay-at-home mom. It was very lonely. I was with a newborn all day, alone with my thoughts. I felt needed in ways that exacerbated my irritability. I would text my friends, but they were usually working, so I didn't get many responses throughout the day. The loneliness started to suck the life out of me like a dementor.

Every day felt like the day before. Wake up, feed the baby, make breakfast, feed the baby, clean, feed the baby, make lunch, clean while the baby naps, feed the baby, go to the park and pretend to look for a mom friend, feed the baby, start dinner, and feed the baby. When my husband got home, I felt too guilty to ask for help because he was working all day. Who was I to ask him for some "me" time? So, I fed the baby while he relaxed. By 8 p.m., I was mentally and physically drained. One day I woke up and cried. As my daughter was cooing in the early hours of the morning, I just sat down next to her crib, head in my hands, and cried. I was crying because I knew something was wrong. But I cried harder because my solution was to take my life.

I was supposed to be happy! But I wasn't. I didn't understand why I felt the way that I did. I don't recall anyone in my family talking about feeling lonely and sad after having a baby. They said it would be hard, but they didn't say anything about feeling suicidal. The last time I had been suicidal, I had just graduated from my bachelor's program. I didn't take my life because I always believed God wouldn't forgive me and I would go to hell. I don't like being hot, so the thought of spending eternity in hell without any water or AC felt like suicide wasn't worth it. So, I kept going. I kept pretending I was happy. I kept socializing. And I just kept going.

In keeping going, I tried to make friends and practice self-care. No one tells you as an adult how hard it is to make new friends. Although I was a SAHM, I worked part-time in the evenings two nights a week. The highlight of my week was going into work for my four-hour shift. My life was going according to plan. But on the inside, there was this pain that went unhealed.

When I started to consider how my daughter would feel growing up and knowing that her mommy died by suicide, I thought to myself, "You're skating on thin ice with these thoughts." So, I reached out to some friends. While I was waiting for them to reply, I remember thinking, "I want to die, and I hope they know that responding is what could save my life." And that's when I knew it was time to give therapy a try.

I found myself struggling to find a Black therapist. But honestly, my life was at stake, and I needed to see someone ASAP. So, I found someone who had an immediate opening. I remember driving to the office feeling ecstatic and thinking, "This could save my life." That's all I wanted. When I sat down, I knew right away that this woman was not the therapist for me. But I reminded myself, "We are here to save your life." I made myself go. I showed up to every appointment. I didn't dislike her, and she did provide the space for me to talk. We just didn't vibe. Back then I didn't know what the relationship between a therapist and client was supposed to look like. The more I went, the less I wanted to die by suicide. The more I went, the less lonely I felt. I knew, every other week this lady would listen to me, validate me, and support me, and that was what I needed.

What if I had never gone to therapy? What if I hadn't stayed with that therapist? Although she wasn't a good fit all around, she did give me what I needed at that time. That imperfect therapeutic relationship was enough to kick-start my healing journey. And because of that, I get to help you start yours. I am here today to talk to you, as a therapist, about dope therapy. I want you to ask yourself: "What is the risk if I don't heal?"

HOW TO USE THIS BOOK

I wrote this book because I wanted to offer an informed and down-to-earth resource for getting the most benefit from therapy. It is filled with information to help you navigate the murky waters of the therapeutic relationship, from understanding trauma to doing the work, and everything in between. There are two ways that you can read this book.

As a self-help guide in navigating your therapy journey. If you're considering therapy but don't know where to start, reading this book from start to finish will help you better understand how the process works and will guide you through each step of the therapy journey. It will let you know what to expect and what to look out for as you begin therapy.

As an à la carte companion to your therapy journey. If you've already embarked on your therapy journey, you can dip into this book as needed. Refer to the table of contents to find the chapter that addresses what you're experiencing during therapy. For instance, if you're not vibing with your therapist, you may visit Chapter 5: Your Relationship with Your Therapist. Or maybe you're not sure if therapy is working. Chapter 11: Is Therapy Helping? can help with that.

Along the way, you'll be introduced to some scenarios with fictional clients, each of whom is working through different issues in therapy. These individuals are fictionalized characters, but the issues they're dealing with are based on real problems. You may find that some of their struggles resonate with your experiences.

» **Jordan:** A proud, gay Black man. In therapy, he is contemplating his eight-year relationship and looking to address feelings of loneliness.

» **Muranda:** A Black female social worker who is married with two kids. Her marriage is on the verge of a divorce, which is why she is seeking therapy. Her therapy work is focusing on boundaries, her anxious attachment, and feeling overwhelmed.

- » **Quinn**: A nonbinary Black individual. They struggle with irritability and sleep.

- » **Gemma**: An older Black woman who is trying to find ways to assert herself.

- » **Yara**: A young Asian woman who is struggling with forgiveness and healing after her recent breakup.

- » **George:** A Hispanic male, age 33, who is working on healing his anxious-avoidant attachment style.

- » **Joshua**: A Black man from Illinois who is struggling with trauma from his childhood.

- » **Tu:** A young Vietnamese woman who was adopted and is working on defining her identity.

Throughout the book, you'll also meet some **Dope Experts**. These are mental health professionals or professionals who specialize in specific areas and have lent their expertise to this book.

- » **Berna Anat** is a self-described Financial Hype Woman who teaches millennials about finances while twerking. She'll take you through getting your money situation in check to afford therapy.

- » **Dr. Kojo Sarfo** specializes in psychiatric medications and ADHD. His work on social media focuses on the less common symptoms of ADHD and depression.

- » **Dr. Courtney Tracy (a.k.a The Truth Doctor)** brings her no #BS approach to to therapy. Her belief is that we are human first.

- » **Dr. Kristen Casey** is a psychologist and sleep clinician. She uses her platforms to educate people on how to create better sleep hygiene.

- » **Dr. Desta** holds a PhD in Clinical Psychology. She is a queer therapist who specializes in trauma, boundaries, and LGBTQ+ issues.

» **Krista Jorgenson MA, LPCC** has extensive experience treating anxiety, depression, borderline personality disorder, trauma, attachment disorders, and LGBTQ+ issues.

» **John Jankord MA, LMFT, LADC, LPCC** works with adolescents, adults, couples, and families using collaborative, solution-focused, person-centered, trauma-focused mindfulness and narrative practices.

Finally, keep a pen and paper handy for the **Dope Exercises** that you'll find in most chapters. These exercises offer opportunities to reflect on your experiences in therapy and get the most from your time with your therapist.

And with that, we begin . . .

CHAPTER ONE

DOPE THERAPY

"The battles that count aren't the ones for gold medals. The struggles within yourself—the invisible, inevitable battles inside all of us—that's where it's at."

—JESSE OWENS

The first time I went to therapy, I was a junior in college. I loved the distraction that drinking gave me from my functioning depression. But I hated the feelings that followed me home the morning after. I felt ashamed, fragile, and suicidal. Those feelings—piled on top of childhood trauma, abandonment issues, and a lack of self-worth—led me straight to the therapy office on my college campus. My suicidal thoughts had become so increasingly overwhelming that I knew that I was going to commit suicide if I didn't talk to someone.

I didn't actually want to take my life, but the pain from all this shit was too much to bear. Something had to die off. It was me or the pain. The pain felt like it was suffocating me and closing in on my life expectancy. Most of my suicidal thoughts came after drinking five to seven UV Lemonades and throwing back several lemon drop shots. At the end of the night, I would lie on the floor of my bathroom, curled up and convulsively crying with a bottle of aspirin in my hand.

Therapy was free in college back in 2006. (I mean, that's the least they could do for the thousands of dollars I paid to take Gen Ed classes like TV broadcasting and humanities.) I made an appointment with the first available therapist. All I knew was that you talk to a therapist when you aren't feeling right.

When I first sat down in the therapist's office, I felt relieved that I was going to be getting help. I was excited that I would get to divulge all the shit I had been holding on to since I was 14. I was ready to trauma-dump like Bob the Builder. The therapist went over therapy protocols and then started with the infamous "So, what brings you in today?" Nonchalantly I said, "I'm fucking a lot of dudes, and no one loves me, but I want to be loved." I said it with a smile on my face, very incongruent with how I was feeling on the inside. On the inside, I was feeling insignificant, exposed, and anxious. But I always appeased my depression with a smile. "Tell me more," she said. Not really knowing what she wanted to hear, I just rambled. And then, just like that, the session was over.

I went back to my dorm, and I thought to myself, *That was wack.* Underwhelming and insignificant. I didn't go back to therapy for another seven years. Looking back, I realize I didn't know that I could choose my therapist, or even that I might have to see several therapists before I found the right one. I didn't know that how I felt leaving the session was a part of the process. I didn't know what expectations I had of therapy, but I did know that what happened wasn't right for me. I felt even more shamed and damaged after the session. Yet I walked away from that experience with a greater season of purpose: to change my major from theater to psychology.

If I couldn't find a therapist to vibe with, I knew I couldn't be the only person feeling that way. That's what led me to getting my master's degree in Educational Psychology and eventually to becoming a Licensed Professional Clinical Counselor in Minnesota.

My bad, I should probably introduce myself. I am Shani Tran, a Licensed Professional Clinical Counselor in Minnesota and a Licensed Professional Counselor in Arizona. I strive to create a safe place for you to own your mental health journey. I do this by dancing on TikTok and sharing vulnerable life lessons on Instagram. I have been in the mental health field since I was 18 years old; I'm currently 35. (If you see me on social media, you will probably say, "You don't look 35!" Yes, yes, I know—Black don't crack! But my husband would prefer you not gas me up too much.)

Over the course of my career, I have looked to define therapy outside of what we see portrayed on TV and social media and in academia. The stereotype we often see is a patient sitting on a couch and a therapist listening without really caring and asking, "How does that make you feel?" Therapy is so much more than that; it's actually pretty dope. I am not referring to your recreational pharmacist's definition of dope. I am referring to the urban slang version of dope. The slang version of "dope" means good, excellent, or nice, and can be used to describe basically anything. For example, "Yo, those shoes are DOooooPE!" or "What you did for me the other day was dope."

When I use "dope" and "therapy" together, I am referring to the positivity that comes from committing to the therapy process. From the good that can come from healing to the amazing relationship that you build with your therapist. You don't have many other opportunities in life to build a relationship with another person that is purely for your benefit. Now that's a win. Know that therapy is a process that you choose (unless it's court ordered, of course).

For therapy to be dope, both you and your therapist must choose to show up authentically. The therapist shows up aware that they're the most important tool in the room. They bring understanding of who they are as a person to the space and allow themselves to be true to that. They are open to your honesty. They go with what feels right, but they don't inflict harm. Sometimes that means letting go of the "shoulds" of what it means to be a therapist so that we can truly see you. For example, in my graduate program, we were taught therapists shouldn't touch clients to avoid sexual assault lawsuits. Yet, if a client asks if they can hug me, and I feel comfortable, I consent. The dopeness of being a therapist is not letting the shoulds of therapy cloud the human experience.

And guess what? *You* also get to choose how you want to show up in therapy. That means what you get from it is dependent upon what you put into it. To engage in the dopeness of therapy, this requires—yes, *requires*—you to show up authentically. But what does it mean for you to show up? It means that you take it session by session, and that you are honest with yourself and your therapist throughout. You may not always know what you want from therapy, but you usually know why you started going to therapy. You want a better understanding of the why of an issue. Being honest means being forthcoming about how you are feeling about the past, present, and future. If a therapist says something you don't vibe with, check them. If you don't want to talk about something, let your therapist know. If your therapist says something that offends you or makes you feel uncomfortable, Let. Them. Know. What is most important is that you have made the choice to go to therapy and to own your healing journey.

Some people avoid therapy because of the accountability that comes with it. Being called out on your shit is tough. Feedback can be hard to take because it can feel like a threat to who you are, and technically it is. But here's the thing: you go to therapy to change. Learning to receive feedback in therapy is a great way to improve the way you show up in life. Hearing feedback from your therapist promotes personal growth. Your therapist will be able to see blind spots in your life that you may not otherwise see. In addition, hearing feedback can be motivating. It tells you that change is not only possible, but also within your control, and it gives you guidance in the areas you need to work on.

Part of dope therapy is recognizing how we play a role in our struggles. You had no control over someone hurting you, but you do have control over how you react, show up in life, and heal. Being called out in a healthy way and taking feedback helps you grow.

I'm guessing you are reading this book because you want to grow. Here are some of the responses I received on Instagram when I asked why people would read a book about therapy.

WHY WOULD YOU WANT TO READ A BOOK ABOUT THERAPY?

To help get insight on what to expect or how to push myself to continue therapy

To learn more about why I think what I think and how I act and the same for other people

Because I can't afford health care or actual therapy

Self-Growth

Because TRAUMA

I would read a book on therapy to educate myself and break stereotypes I have about it

I want to know how to navigate the system and look out for myself; what to expect and what not to expect

To become a better therapist

THE STIGMA AROUND THERAPY

Part of the reality is that therapy is still stigmatized. People still don't go to therapy because they aren't always aware of what to expect from the process. People often have misconceptions about what therapy is. Raise your hand if you have ever heard or said any of these statements: "Therapy is for crazy people," "Therapy isn't affordable," or "I don't have depression; why would I need to go to therapy?" All of these statements are true to the person saying them, as they represent specific schema regarding therapy. A *schema* provides a foundation to organize the world around you. You have schemas about yourself, events, social interactions, family, work, and animals. Just about everything has a schema. Schemas are developed throughout your life experiences and then stored to access when you need to interpret a situation, a person, or the world around you. Schemas influence your emotions, behaviors, memories, and thoughts.

CAT SCHEMA

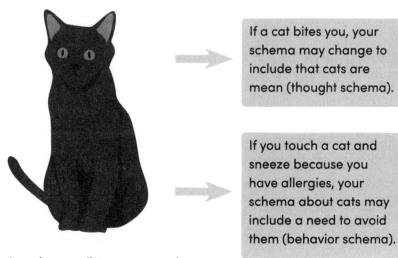

If a cat bites you, your schema may change to include that cats are mean (thought schema).

If you touch a cat and sneeze because you have allergies, your schema about cats may include a need to avoid them (behavior schema).

A cat has a tail, two ears, and is furry.

Although schemas can help you navigate the world, they can also be harmful if you aren't aware of them. Schemas about therapy can lead to internalized stigma. For example, you may have a schema that only people with severe mental health conditions attend therapy. Let's say you witnessed Cousin Peaches going in and out of therapy due to heroin addiction. At some point, you overheard your mother comment that therapy doesn't work because Peaches is still a lying piece of shit who steals. (I know; family can be cruel.) You may have developed two schemas: therapy doesn't work, and you are a piece of shit if you struggle with mental health. As an adult, you now find yourself needing therapy. You feel guilty, ashamed, and shitty at your first appointment. Why? Because you are navigating around the negative messages about therapy and applying them to yourself. That is internalized stigma.

EVENT	SCHEMA	
Your friend tells you they went to therapy and it didn't work.	THERAPY DOESN'T WORK	**Emotion** → Annoyed **Thoughts** → Therapy is a waste of time **Behaviors** → Don't go to therapy **Body Sensation** → Tense

The impacts of internalized stigma can be detrimental to your therapy process. Because of your internalized stigma around therapy and mental health, you can find yourself struggling with low self-esteem, believing in stereotypes, using maladaptive coping skills, and experiencing increased symptoms of mental health conditions. But what if you're stronger than that and still choose to seek out therapy? Internalized stigma can show up in sessions when you hold back on your thoughts and emotions.

There are a lot of negative messages around what therapy is, which lead to misconceptions that can validate your negative schemas around therapy. Let's take a look at these misconceptions and reframe them into healthier thoughts.

WHAT YOU HEARD ABOUT THERAPY	DOPE THERAPY
It is for the weak and crazy.	Therapy is for anyone who wants to implement change in their life.
Instead of listening, therapists just take notes while you sit on a couch.	Therapists take notes and listen. We take notes because we want to remember important things about you. Therapy comes in different forms, such as play and dance therapy.
It's just talking.	In therapy you don't always have to talk; silence can be powerful. But yes, the most common form of therapy is talking. You talk about something so that you can process it and figure out how to change it.
You get blamed.	A therapist can help you take accountability over your life. As a child, you had no control over what happened to you, and now you get to control how you heal. This can lead to choices in who you interact with, how you interact with people, and what boundaries you put in place.
A therapist is a paid friend.	I would love to be friends with some of my clients, but then I couldn't be their therapist. Friends give advice, whereas a therapist helps guide you toward making healthy decisions on your own. (More on this in Chapter 5.)
It's only for people with serious mental health conditions.	Absolutely the F not! Therapy is for people who want to make a change. That's it. Want to change the way you feel about your self-esteem? Therapy. Want to change careers? Therapy. Want to improve your relationships? Therapy.

Our views on therapy are often influenced by how our family talks about therapy. I want you to take a moment and think about what you were told about therapy growing up. Some Black people are told, "Going to therapy is some white people shit." It was not typical for a Black person of my parents' generation to be sitting in a therapy waiting room. One reason for this is that therapy is taught using a Westernized approach. Honestly, as a Black woman, I can't think of many psychology theories that are representative of me. Imagine trying to find a therapist that not only looks like you, but also has a therapy approach that's flavored with cultural understanding, empathy toward generational trauma, and #blackthanksgivingclapbacks (Iykyk). "You don't tell nobody yo' business" is still a generational curse that many Black people are trying to unlearn. We also can't forget the history of trauma for Black people in America, with the reality being that the field is still majority white. (Or, as TikTok would say, "YT people.")

Schemas around situations can be created from how we see others react to situations. Throughout the book, I use fictional characters in scenarios to better explain how a certain topic may present itself in therapy. Meet our first character, Muranda.

Muranda is 35 years old and struggling in her marriage. She heard about how therapy had helped a coworker heal her marriage. But Muranda is plagued by her family's experience with therapy. When she was 13, her father left shortly after starting therapy with her mother. Afterward, her mother blamed the divorce on therapy and often said, "Therapy ruined my marriage and me." Muranda is unaware that her father's affair had been revealed to her mom during a therapy session. She remembers her mother's angry and dismissive reaction whenever friends and family would ask how therapy was going. Muranda is confused about whether therapy can help. Her thought schema around therapy is that it doesn't work and only makes things worse. However, hearing about her coworker's experience with therapy is challenging her schema.

FEAR OF THE UNKNOWN

Going to therapy may be unknown for you. When we come up against the unknown, our brains can react out of fear. Fear can keep us safe, but it can also hinder us from growth. Have you ever stayed in a situation because you didn't know what it would be like outside of that situation? This situation could be a relationship, a job, or even not speaking up when you wanted to.

That's where we meet Jordan. Jordan is 32, biracial, and a proud G of the LGBTQ+ community. Jordan wants things to change in his relationship, which is his reason for seeking therapy. However, he is worried about what could happen if he goes to therapy. He has never been to therapy and he is not sure of what to expect.

> Jordan has been with his partner for eight years. In the beginning, things were great. It was the first time he took things slow in a relationship. According to him, he did everything right. He found out their attachment styles, learned their love languages, and even waited for a commitment before sleeping together. Then, about six years into the relationship, he started feeling lonely and disconnected from his partner. This led to increased irritability and unhappiness that leaked into other parts of Jordan's life, leaving him feeling invalidated, unloved, and tempted to cheat. Leaving is not an option because they have been together for too long and he knows there's potential if he can just stick it out. The loneliness soon exacerbates into isolation, and Jordan withdraws from his partner. Jordan doesn't attend therapy because he's unsure and worried about the outcomes. So, he continues to be unhappy. Yes, he knows things could get better if he goes to therapy, but he fears the worst. What if he realizes he no longer wants to be with his partner? What will happen in therapy is unknown and he can't predict the outcome, so for now he chooses not to go.

If you have never experienced therapy, it can fall into the unknown. The unknown is one of the four threats to the brain. (The other three are physical/emotional safety, incongruence in the environment, and when we "should" ourselves.) The unknown is a threat because when we encounter new experiences, our brains search through past information to give us an insight into new experiences. When this happens, our brains tend to hyperfocus on things that are similar to the new experience but didn't go well.

If you have never been to therapy, you don't know what to expect or what the outcome will be. And because you have never been to therapy, your brain is pulling from past information to help make an assumption about a predictable outcome. As your brain hyperfocuses on the negative, you may perceive the outcome as negative. Your brain may assess therapy as a threat. What if you go to therapy and it gets worse, or even better? You don't know what worse or better looks like.

As you are trying to make a decision around going to therapy, you may feel increasingly anxious and worried. Your uncertainty about the situation is guiding your decision-making. Ask yourself instead: What if this goes well and ends up being a dope experience? What if therapy helps you? What do those possibilities around therapy look like? What if you find a therapist you vibe with? This is a great way to challenge your fear of the unknown. The truth is, you don't know, so your fearful thoughts at the moment are assumptions.

Challenging your thoughts means evaluating the evidence. Ask yourself: Even though I am fearful of therapy, if I have never gone, where's the evidence that it won't help? If you have a friend who is in therapy and it's working for them, it may be helpful to reach out and ask them about their experiences. Research what to expect from therapy—you already have a head start by reading this book!—and then practice radical acceptance, and accept that therapy is unknown for you. By evaluating the evidence and learning about therapy, you are increasing your tolerance to the unknown. Look at you! You just learned how to challenge your thoughts in a healthy way.

AM I READY FOR THERAPY?

You're thinking about going to therapy. I see you! Let's talk about how you know if you're ready. The first thing is that you're already aware that you need help navigating things in your life. You have a sense that something is amiss. You may not be sure of where to go from here, but you feel things need to change. Maybe, up until now, you felt at a standstill and struggled to break unhealthy habits. You had no control over your childhood or the hurt that people inflicted on you. But now you do have control over your story. And this type of control can feel pretty awesome. Therapy is not a monolith. Knowing whether therapy is right for you can be challenging. Here are some reasons that you may see a therapist and what dope therapy can do for you.

REASONS TO SEE A THERAPIST	DOPE THERAPY CAN HELP YOU . . .
You struggle to regulate your emotions.	Identify, label, and regulate your emotions and feel more in control of them.
You've noticed changes in sleep, appetite, or energy.	Recognize where the changes are coming from and learn healthy ways to improve them.
You struggle with school or work.	Gain insight into the origination of the struggle and increase performance in these areas.
You struggle with personal relationships, such as those with friends, family, or a partner.	Learn and implement effective communication skills, assertiveness, and enhanced social skills.

REASONS TO SEE A THERAPIST	DOPE THERAPY CAN HELP YOU . . .
You no longer take pleasure in activities you used to enjoy.	Regain joy in your life, whether that is by returning to a previously enjoyed activity or by starting a new one.
You experienced a loss or a death.	Gain understanding around loss, whether it is the loss of a job, the death of someone in your life, or the loss of your rights. If it meant a lot to you and is no longer in your life, therapy can help you grieve.
You want to become a better you.	Pinpoint the areas of your life where you want to improve, determine how to go about it, and provide you with a safe place to practice this improvement.
You've had a decline in physical health.	Gain clarity around how your life has been impacted by your physical health and help give you a greater sense of control over your physical health.
You have difficulty coping.	Identify what isn't working and learn healthy coping skills that enhance your life.
You've experienced trauma.	Talk about the shitty things that have happened to you while also supporting you as you adapt to how you have been changed by the traumatic situation. Go from victim to survivor.
You're dealing with addiction.	Understand addiction and how you have been impacted by it. Learn how to control your behaviors and actions. Gain insight into the root causes to bring awareness to your triggers. Offer efficacious methods to overcome addiction.

Many of us do not learn how to be aware of ourselves. This includes physical, emotional, and mental awareness. We might find ourselves struggling because we feel out of control. And when we feel out of control, we sometimes turn to *maladaptive coping skills* to help "get us through." Maladaptive coping skills can help us feel better in the short term but affect us negatively in the long term. An example could be emotional eating. You had a rough day at work, so you go straight for the pint of Jeni's ice cream in the freezer when you get back home. (Top shelf, in the back, on the right—Jeni's ice cream does hit different, though.) You find that you feel better. Just for the moment, Jeni's gooey creaminess satiates your need to escape and be happy. Then you realize that you've started to put on some weight. And then, maybe not immediately, but after eating the ice cream, you feel as empty as the pint in front of you. The feeling before the maladaptive coping skill comes back, maybe stronger than before. Because you weren't dealing with the cause of your emotions, eating the ice cream only helped temporarily. In addition, it led to gaining weight, which has led to a decrease in self-esteem. You coped, but not in a healthy way.

Maladaptive coping skills are behaviors that might alleviate stress or make you feel better in the moment, but ultimately have a negative impact on your life. Examples include:

▶ Avoidance

▶ Substance use

▶ Self-harm

▶ Emotional eating

▶ Passive aggressiveness

▶ Compulsive lying

After years of suffering from low self-esteem and an inability to quit emotional eating, you find yourself browsing the *Psychology Today* site looking for a therapist. You figure a therapist will be able to help you find the trigger to your emotional eating. A *trigger* is when you have an intense emotional reaction to something. It can be a memory, person, place, or thing. We have to name it so we can tame it. We can't stop the emotional eating with just skills; we need to know the root cause.

You can go to therapy to find the root cause of anything. Take a moment and ask yourself: "Is there something that I am struggling with in life right now?" "Is there something going on in my life that I stay up late thinking about?" It's not just about what made you fall, fail, or cry. It is also how you pick yourself up. You are capable of doing it. I know you are capable of doing it because you're reading this book. This tells me that you are motivated to go to therapy, or at least interested.

Sometimes we "should" on ourselves. We should on ourselves when we place pressure to do or be something else. It makes us feel less than. Raise your hand if you have ever should on yourself. When you should on yourself, you are expecting yourself to be someone you are not. Take a moment to think about a "should" you have said to yourself. "I should work this job for two to three years because that's how you move up the corporate ladder." "I should be grateful." "I should be humble." "I should not speak up because that would hurt the other person's feelings." When you make statements with "should," and there's a pressure to be someone you're not, you are betraying your authentic self. If you no longer want to be burdened by the threats of shoulds, therapy can help.

The only person who can decide if therapy is right for you is you. What is important is to acknowledge that you are thinking about going.

DOPE EXERCISE: IS THERAPY FOR ME?

If you're considering therapy, ask yourself . . .

- *Why do I want to go to therapy?*
- *Why don't I want to go to therapy?*
- *What have I heard about therapy?*
- *If I go to therapy, how will I know it is working?*
- *If I decide not to go to therapy and nothing changes, am I okay with that?*

To help identify your emotions related to going to therapy, turn to the list of emotions provided at the end of this chapter. Scan through them, and choose any that resonate with you.

Not everyone is ready for therapy. Choosing not to go to therapy at this time is valid and okay. And at the same time, not everyone who wants to go to therapy is ready for the process. There might be some telltale signs that show you are not ready for therapy. The first indicator may be that you intentionally schedule an appointment that is several weeks out. If the therapist has earlier openings and you choose an appointment that is more than two weeks out, this may be a sign that you aren't ready. The same falls for appointment times. For example, you find a therapist whose profile you vibe with, but you choose not to go to them because they don't work weekends. I want you to pause and ask yourself why. We make time for dentists, doctors, eye exams, and other appointments during the week. Why not therapy? Or maybe you make an appointment and don't show up. This could be a one-off situation. But if you have put in the time and work to research a therapist and you choose not to show up, this may mean now is not a good time for you.

What themes do you notice here? Time and importance. When therapy feels like it is infringing on your time, it is not important to you. Let's own that. If you aren't honest with yourself about where you are in your healing journey, therapy can be harmful. Whenever a new client starts therapy, I always inform them that sometimes things can get worse before they get better. Your symptoms could increase, you may talk about things you've never told anyone, and sometimes the dependency on your therapist increases. If you start therapy when you aren't ready, you may end up dropping out when things get tough. And then you can find yourself in a worse place than you were before. Or maybe you are ready. Just like there are signs that you aren't ready for therapy, there are things to look for that may indicate you are ready.

YOU MAY BE READY FOR THERAPY IF . . .

- **You read self-help books.** Are you that person who has read self-help books to try to implement new skills in your life?

- **You are aware that something is affecting you.** Something is off and causing distress, *and* you don't want to feel that way anymore.

- **You look at your bank account to see if you could afford therapy.** You've already started to think about how you can make therapy happen.

- **You're in pain.** You're feeling pain in some area of your life and want to gain insight and clarification.

- **You want to be a more authentic you.** The *shoulda woulda couldas* are getting on your damn nerves.

- **You are open to the therapy process.** You are looking forward to being open and honest with yourself while being guided by a therapist.

If some of those reasons jumped out at you, you may be ready. Or you fall into the category of someone who is already in therapy and looking for further guidance. If you're thinking, "I need some dope therapy in my life," you have one of the most powerful indicators of a successful and dope therapy journey: wanting to begin or wanting to continue. I get a lot of comments on my TikTok videos from people asking how they can get someone they love to go to therapy. I always say that need is not a requirement, but wanting to go is. Wanting to go to therapy means that you are more likely to be motivated to implement what you learn from the process. Being motivated by why you want to go to therapy is what will help guide you through. The motivation to want to go to therapy is paramount, not just for setting your goals for therapy, but also for creating and sustaining behaviors aimed at completing your goals in therapy.

When you make the choice to go to therapy, you take accountability of your narrative and healing process. You get to do the work, and no one can take that away from you. You'll learn about how you became the person you are so that you can show up as the person you want to be. When you know more about why you think the way you think and behave the way you behave, you can now make empowering and cognizant choices through awareness.

Dope therapy empowers you to be genuine to the process that is ahead. This is your journey—embrace and own that. Once you find a dope therapist, you are no longer alone in your healing. You now have someone in your corner who is rooting for you to succeed in the dopest way. Your therapist will validate, support, and empower you, all while calling you out on your shit to increase accountability. They want to see you not just grow, but also overcome challenges. And when you feel like uphill growth is impossible, all you have to do is look in front of you because there's your therapist wearing an invisible shirt that says, "Go Team You!"

DOPE TAKEAWAYS

» When you show up authentically as yourself to therapy, you reap the benefits.

» Schemas are developed from life experiences. Your schemas around therapy can prevent you from healing.

» The unknown can be frightening because you can't predict the outcome.

» Stigma takes many forms; you have to ask yourself what you believe.

» Maladaptive coping may help in the moment, but it is unhealthy in the long term.

» Truly assess whether you are ready for therapy or not; starting the process when you're not ready can be harmful.

» You may not have control over those who hurt you, but you can take responsibility for your healing.

EMOTIONS LIST

A
angry
annoyed
afraid
awkward
anxious
aggravated
apprehensive
ashamed
abandoned

B
brave
bothered
bitter

C
cheerful
confident
calm
cold
content
cranky
concerned
crushed
compulsive

D
defiant
depressed
discouraged
disgusted
determined
disappointed
disengaged

E
elated
enthusiastic
embarrassed
excited
exhausted
eager

F
frightened
fearful
furious
fatigued

G
grouchy
guilty
glad
gooey
grateful

H
happy
humiliated
hurt
helpless
hopeless
hyperactive

I
irritated
irritable
insecure
inadequate
isolated

J
judged
joyful

L
lethargic
lazy

M
mad
miserable
manipulated
misunderstood

N
nasty
nervous
neglected
neglectful
numb

O
obsessive
overstimulated
optimistic

P
panicked
peaceful
powerless
pleased
petty
proud

R
relieved
relaxed
rational
restless

S
sad
surprised
scared
shy
sensitive
safe
stubborn
secure
satisfied

T
tearful
tired
torn

U
unhappy
unsure
uneasy
uncertain
uncomfortable

V
violent
valued
vulnerable
victimized

CHAPTER TWO

THE BUSINESS OF THERAPY

"You will either step forward into growth or step back into safety."

—ABRAHAM MASLOW

Whether we like it or not, therapy operates as a business. Understanding the business aspect of therapy can help you feel empowered as you navigate insurance, paperwork, and even the diagnosis process. When it comes to your mental health, being educated on the different processes can help you make well-informed decisions. I hope this chapter gives what it's supposed to give: education and empowerment.

The cost of therapy can often make it feel out of reach. I think about the Black person who believes that therapy is only for wealthy white people. Or the person seeking therapy for gender-affirming care who finds that qualified therapists are out of network. Or the person desperately in search of affordable therapy services.

UNDERSTANDING THERAPY RATES

Therapists are typically paid by the session, and most therapists have session lengths of 30 to 60 minutes. While the rate per session may seem high, it's important to keep in mind that therapists put in additional work outside of the face-to-face time with a client that is not billed. They spend time typing up notes, researching clinical approaches and strategies, consulting with colleagues, and processing invoices and billing. All these tasks take place outside of billable time.

Also, therapists who accept insurance must meet certain parameters when billing. To bill for a 60-minute session, the therapist must spend a minimum of 53 minutes with the client. Consider this scenario: Yara, who uses insurance, is running late to her therapy appointment, so she calls her therapist to let them know. Her appointment started at 4 p.m., but she arrives at 4:11 p.m. This leaves 49 minutes in the 60-minute session. The therapist is not allowed to bill for a 60-minute session because Yara has not been face-to-face with the therapist for a minimum of 53 minutes. Instead, the therapist will bill for a 45-minute session. (A 45-minute session is allowed if the face-to-face time falls between 38 and

52 minutes. A 30-minute session is billable for between 16 and 37 minutes of face-to-face time.) You may be thinking, "Why not extend the session?" To make that decision, a few factors come into play. First, is there a client after Yara? If there is, the therapist will need to adhere to the allotted time to respect the client after Yara. If there is no one after Yara, it is at the discretion of the therapist. The therapist may extend Yara's session, or they might use it as an opportunity to practice accountability and not extend the session.

Therapists who accept insurance don't get paid for time outside of being face-to-face with clients because the pay that we receive for the session is meant to cover any additional time spent working on the client's case outside of the session. However, if a client shows up late, that doesn't mean the work is less. It just means less time was spent with the client. Therapists who use a self-pay model get to set their rates to compensate for time outside the session. In addition, self-paying clients may be charged for the entire session regardless of arriving late.

WHAT DOES INSURANCE ACCESS MEAN?

Most people prefer to use insurance to pay for therapy services. However, I often find that clients aren't informed on all the pros and cons of using insurance. Most Americans have never been told to question their healthcare benefits or to inquire what it means to use them. We sign up for health insurance plans and usually pay attention to what is included and overall costs, but we haven't been taught to ask about what it means to use your insurance to pay for mental health services.

I think we can agree that a pro to using insurance is having access to a network of providers who specialize in services to help us. But what does access really mean? When you sign up for an insurance policy, you will have access to therapists who accept your health insurance. Your insurance provider has a database of therapists with whom they have contracts. Therapists have the freedom to choose which insurance contracts they sign; however, some insurance companies don't allow new contracts because they are at capacity with the number of contracts they have in place and don't always assess for access to different populations.

If you are white and cisgender, you have much greater accessibility than someone who is a Black Indigenous Person of Color (BIPOC). When I started my private practice, one of the largest insurance companies denied me. The response was that they had enough contracts with therapists in my area. I wrote them an appeal letter emphasizing that they didn't have enough contracts with *Black therapists.* I explained how that negatively impacted the mental health of the Black community by limiting Black people's access to in-network therapists. That insurance company then offered me a contract.

The limitations of finding a therapist who is in network can dramatically decrease the likelihood that individuals from minority communities will seek and receive mental health services. Yes, using insurance lowers the cost of therapy, but it can also limit access to a therapist who fits other needs like gender identity, ethnicity, language, and culture. Why is that? Due to freedom in setting their own prices, more and more therapists are moving to self-pay. If you have struggled to find an in-network therapist, it may be beneficial to expand your search out of network. We will discuss this later in the chapter.

UNDERSTANDING INSURANCE: CO-PAYS, COINSURANCE, AND DEDUCTIBLES

What is the difference between a co-pay, coinsurance, and a deductible? A *co-pay* is a fixed amount that you pay your therapist every time you see them. Co-pays are usually low and keep therapy affordable. Coinsurance? She can be straight up rude; she means that you pay a certain percentage of the bill. This could look like your insurance covering 30 percent of the bill and you paying the remaining 70 percent. If you have a deductible, you are responsible for paying all your healthcare bills until you reach a certain amount. Say your deductible is $1,000; this means you pay $1,000 out of pocket before your insurance starts to cover the costs.

If you have coinsurance or a deductible, you can ask the therapist about your insurance benefits and what their contracted rate is with your insurance provider to know what you'd be expected to pay. If the therapist can't answer the question, you can also call your insurance company and ask about your mental health benefits. The insurance company will also be able to tell you where you are as far as reaching your deductible if you have one.

> *Muranda wants to start couples counseling. She calls the insurance company and learns that her plan has a coinsurance of 50/50 with an out-of-pocket maximum of $7,000. Feeling informed, Muranda emails a therapist to set up her first couples counseling appointment. Muranda feels that it will take more than 60 minutes to cover several years of unaddressed issues, so she asks for a 90-minute session in her email. When the therapist responds, Muranda is taken aback to find out couples therapy isn't covered by her insurance and neither are 90-minute sessions. The therapist explains that if she would like a 90-minute session, the self-pay rate is $225. Furthermore, a 60-minute session at the insurance contracted rate is $140. This means that she would have to pay $70 per session, because her coinsurance is 50/50, until her out-of-pocket maximum of $7,000 is met for the year. In addition, she can bring her spouse, but Muranda would be considered the client. Muranda has a few choices. She can pay the self-pay rate for extended sessions. Or she can use her insurance and have 60-minute sessions. Or she can continue to shop around for a different self-pay rate for 90-minute sessions.*

DOPE EXERCISE: WHAT TO ASK YOUR INSURANCE

Before using your insurance to cover therapy, call and ask the following questions.

- *Are mental health services covered under my plan?*

- *What are my choices for choosing a professional, such as a psychologist or master's-level therapist?*

- *Do I have a co-pay? If so, what is it?*

- *Do I have coinsurance? If so, what is it?*

- *Do I have a deductible? What counts toward my deductible? When does the deductible amount start over again?*

- *Is there a limit to the number of sessions covered by insurance?*

- *Is there an Employee Assistance Program (EAP)? (Cha-ching . . . free sessions! More on EAPs in Chapter 3.)*

UNDERSTANDING INSURANCE: THE THERAPIST NETWORK

It was recently time for my yearly pap smear and I was nervous AF. Mainly because my last OBGYN was amazing, but I moved to Arizona from Minnesota and needed to find a new one. I wanted to find an OBGYN who was a woman of color, so I took to the innanets to find someone that I could comfortably discuss my vaginal health with. One stood out; she looked so dope, but she didn't accept my insurance. *Dammit, she's out of network.* This sucked for me because I didn't have out-of-network benefits. Every insurance plan has in-network benefits, but not all have out-of-network benefits. If a therapist is in network, they have a contract with the insurance company and will accept your insurance as payment for services. If a therapist is out of network, they don't have a contract with the insurance company; therefore, it's important to check if you have out-of-network benefits to cover services.

Why are some therapists out of network? Because different insurance companies have different rates, and some therapists may choose to not accept the insurance due to their rate. Also, the process to become in network with insurance companies can be as long as "The Long Night" episode of *Game of Thrones*. It feels like forever; you're not sure if you will even get a contract; and it's hella time-consuming, roughly three to four months.

If you are wondering whether a therapist accepts your insurance, check their profile on psychologytoday.com. If you don't see your insurance listed on their profile, they more than likely don't accept it. When I was searching for a therapist shortly after my dog passed away in 2020, I struggled to find someone who was in network. I wanted to find someone who looked like me—a Black woman—and with a smile like Halle Berry, but the search pages of psychologytoday.com were saturated with white therapists. There were only a few Black therapists—male or female—and in every case their bio said either "not accepting insurance" or "not accepting new clients."

UNDERSTANDING INSURANCE: DIAGNOSING

Insurance companies operate off a medical model. What this means for clients is that they must be diagnosed if they are using their insurance. The diagnosis must be made during the first session, so the therapist must look for symptoms to meet the criteria for a diagnosis. A diagnosis can give both the client and the therapist insight into what is going on, and it can be helpful, if it is accurate. Therapists use the *Diagnostic and Statistical Manual of Mental Disorders*, Fifth Edition (DSM-5), which outlines criteria for choosing a diagnosis.

There have definitely been times when I have found myself trying to come up with a diagnosis based on the information I've been given by the client in the first session. That's where the diagnosis of adjustment disorder can be a saving grace. In the therapy world, it's a diagnosis we use when struggling to find a diagnosis. This is because behavioral and emotional changes due to an identifiable stressor fulfill the criteria for an adjustment disorder. Who doesn't have stress?!

A therapist who accepts insurance does not get paid unless they diagnose. Sometimes this can be harmful in the first session because rapport is being built and the client may not feel as open and comfortable. But therapists have to make sure they draw out information for a diagnosis, which is why the first session may feel impersonal.

If rapport and trust are lacking, it can lead to a misdiagnosis. The therapist may not have all the information in the first session, and rightfully so. You just met your therapist. A therapist may also misdiagnose because some diagnoses have similar symptoms but differ in duration. For instance, dysthymia (prolonged depression) can be misdiagnosed on the first session if not enough history is gathered. This can affect the client because a misdiagnosis can lead to wrong treatments being recommended and even wrong medications prescribed, if the client is seeing a psychiatrist. (Only a prescribing professional, such as a nurse practitioner, psychiatrist, or a primary care provider, can prescribe medications.)

Even when a diagnosis is made correctly, it may lead to higher life insurance costs or even denial. You could even find yourself with a permanent mental health record, which can affect people when they apply for certain jobs. Even though your information is confidential between you and your therapist, the insurance authorization form that you sign in the first session allows your therapist to share information with your insurance company. The catch is that if you want to use insurance, you must sign the form.

Your insurance company can share your diagnosis with other insurance companies.

Diagnosing is not always negative. It can help to clarify the patient's struggles and to provide guided treatment recommendations for improved mental health. Diagnosing is also helpful because it gives clients a name. When we can name what is going on with us, it allows us to figure out how to solve it. With a proper diagnosis that has been assessed and even tested, the therapist can use different tools to help improve the mental health of their clients. Although there can be risks to having a diagnosis, the success of treating a diagnosis can far outweigh the risks.

This information is used to inform you so that you can make decisions that are best for you. There are some pros to paying for therapy with insurance. One is that you only need to budget for the out-of-pocket costs because your premium comes out of your paycheck. This may be easier and more affordable for you. Sometimes we do things because it's the norm and we didn't know all the risks involved or that there are other options. Know that determining the risks is subjective. If you are reading this and wondering if there is another way, the answer is yes—self-pay.

UNDERSTANDING SELF-PAY

Self-pay therapy can cost upwards of $200 per 50-minute session. What is your reaction to that statement—physically and mentally? How did you feel about that? Surprised, shocked, upset, annoyed, okay with it? Did you just have a Smokey moment and say, DAYYYYUM? Did you think, "Ah, that's not bad, it's much higher where I live"? And where did you feel those feelings? Did your shoulders tense? Did you clench your jaw or furrow your brow? Now I want you to ask yourself: Why do I think I had that reaction? It may be related to what you determine the value of therapy to be. Jay Shetty, life coach and author of *Think Like a Monk*, says, "Everyone is born into a certain set of circumstances, and our values are defined by what we experience." Any mental and/or physical reactions you had are related to your values around money and therapy.

~~~~~~~~~~~~~~~~~~~~~~~~~~~~~~~~~~~

DOPE EXPERT: BERNA ANAT (@heyberna)

To dive further into how money can impact your therapy journey, I thought I would invite a money expert into the conversation. She is not only your internet financial hype woman, but also a person of color. Meet Berna Anat.

> **Girl, as you and I know, therapy isn't always accessible. How can someone who feels they can't afford therapy approach their finances?**

First of all, I'm screaming a collective scream for all of us due to how inaccessible affordable therapy can be. We gotta do a little DIY called exploring your Money Story. Money is not a neutral thing for any of us; everyone grew up with some type of emotional tie, trauma, or trigger around money, particularly in our childhoods, and we carry those into our adult lives.

You can start by thinking back to your earliest money memories. Make some tea, turn on some smooth jazz, grab your favorite free-thinking medium—a journal, a voice note app, even a friend you feel safe with—and conduct a little Money Story self-interview with the following questions:

- What's the first emotion that comes to mind when you think about money? Do you feel any reaction in your body? Do any images come to mind? (Shani taught me this!)

- What is your earliest memory of money? When is the first time you remember being aware of the existence of money in your family? In your household? Among your friends?

- What feelings come up around those memories? Some of our greatest hits: shame ("It was embarrassing not being able to afford things the way my classmates could"); scarcity ("My parents were always telling us how we have no money"); and tension ("My family fought about bills, but we never talked about it outside of the house").

- As a child, what could you have learned about money from those memories? How are those memories or feelings still showing up in your adult life?

Hella different circumstances merged to make your money habits, and many of them were likely out of your control. Financial empathy, baby!

> **I hear you, but what does someone need to pay attention to when it comes to their mindset around money?**

As annoying as it is to hear, dealing with money is a lifelong journey because your financial life will change just as much as your regular life does. Just like any other kind of trauma, reworking our financial habits will never be a straight, linear path. But I hold radical financial empathy for myself. I remind myself that I'm the first in my lineage to even attempt this financial health stuff, and I'm *supposed* to make mistakes. Fun fact—we are all compromised under capitalism, especially folks in marginalized communities, and we're all simply trying to do our best with the financial choices we have.

We often associate worth with how much something costs. After you've done a little DIY on your Money Story, think about therapy and what it's worth in terms of value. I challenge you to ask yourself: What experiences have I had with therapy to determine the value of it? You may fall into one of three categories: 1) you don't see the value in paying self-pay because you've never been to therapy, 2) you have been to therapy using insurance and therefore cannot imagine paying self-pay, or 3) you have been to therapy and your experience is not worth the cost of self-pay.

What if we turn the value to look internally? If you are struggling and find a therapist who can help you not struggle, would that be worth the cost? Our experiences directly affect how we view the value of something. I think of my friend who wanted to be in a committed relationship but struggled to find his person. So, he stopped dating. His experiences with dating had tainted the value of it. But the thing is, he continued to long for and desire a partner. How would he find a partner if he's not dating? If you are struggling in an area of your life and you have recognized that what you are doing is no longer working, you may inevitably need to seek therapy. My friend realized that how he was going about dating was why it wasn't working, so he switched it up. Yes, you can put it off because it might not be the *right* time. But in order to heal in healthy ways, you may eventually come back to needing therapy.

I imagine you may still be wondering why self-pay doesn't have lower rates. Tamara Suttle, owner and founder of Private Practice from the Inside Out, does a great job of discussing the barriers to low rates from a clinical standpoint. One of the barriers is that therapists need to operate their businesses. Operational costs might include continuing education credits, which are required to maintain our licenses; licensing fees; and fees to run electronic healthcare records program; as well as fees such as rent, utilities, internet, etc. That's just to run the business; we also have to survive on our income, from both an operational and a relational standpoint.

Yes, therapy requires operations such as internet and rent, but the basis of a therapy office is to provide services that help you get right with your mental health. Therapists are humans too. We have our own values and worth that we bring to our businesses. Feeling underpaid and overworked can affect how we do our work. And if our work is affected, this can directly impact you as the client.

A self-pay therapist gets to set their rates based on what they feel their services are worth. If a client is running late with a therapist who is self-pay, their rate doesn't decrease based on face-to-face time; instead, the client loses that time to process in the session. The therapist is still paid their hourly rate, unless they have a policy that states differently. Self-pay rates may be higher than insurance rates based on a few reasons: the therapist's specialty, their time in the field, their education, and what they feel is worthy to charge for their services. Some therapists try to make therapy more accessible and affordable through sliding-fee scales. A sliding-fee scale means that there is no set rate, and the cost of the session is determined by the client's income. With this process, therapists are to remain unbiased. We cannot just charge one client one rate and charge another client a different rate; we must prove why in an ethical way. If we can't, we do try to offer help in finding more affordable services. When charging clients different rates, we have to take into account how low we can drop our rates and how many clients we can have at a lower rate and still be operational, and we have to remain ethical and unbiased.

After my dog passed away, I found myself having flashbacks of him passing away in my arms. I needed a therapist ASAP. I decided to prioritize what I wanted in a therapist instead of whether or not they were in my network. Even then, I was frustrated that my queries to Black therapists were met with "not accepting new clients" or no reply. I had to focus on other characteristics, such as specialty and personality.

This was my first time paying for therapy through self-pay, but I immediately felt the difference in my first session. I chose my therapist because her profile mentioned she was a runner and loved Harry Potter, so I already felt a connection in our first session. But there was something about her approach. She spent more time getting to know me as a person and not looking for criteria for a diagnosis. With self-pay, a therapist does not have to diagnose. For me, this felt freeing from the mental health stigma. Rather than asking questions to figure out which diagnosis I fit, she was more interested in me as a person. The difference was uncanny. It felt like I was talking to someone who wanted to see me versus my symptoms. When she created my treatment plan, I was shocked to see it. Y'all, it was only one page and easy to read! As a therapist, I longed for the release from medical model treatment plans. When I do them, they are usually several pages long; full of jargon; and outline the diagnosis, symptoms, goals of treatment, and interventions that will be used. My treatment plan from my self-pay therapist had clear, legible, easy-to-understand goals like, "Client wants to remember the happy memories with her dog instead of the flashbacks." I was amazed by how simple and humanistic it felt.

A therapist who is self-pay doesn't need to use the medical model of therapy. The medical model of therapy is: a client comes to therapy, the therapist must find the diagnosis that explains what is wrong, that diagnosis is viewed as treatable, the therapist must show how they will treat it, and treatment is over once a diagnosis is treated. The reality is that mental health is a lifelong process. Sometimes therapy is used for talking through tough shit that doesn't fit into a diagnosis.

INSURANCE	SELF-PAY
Must use in-network providers	Choice of providers
May be lower cost per session	Higher costs
Must receive a diagnosis because of medical model and not all diagnoses are covered under insurance	Therapist can get to know you before making a diagnosis and developing your treatment plan

INSURANCE	SELF-PAY
Information in sessions is shared with the insurance company	Confidential information stays between you and your therapist (unless it falls under mandated reporting)
May be limited to a certain number of sessions	You can go as much as you and your therapist decide is best
Usually limited to 60-minute sessions	You have the option for longer sessions
Insurance has a factor in deciding if the treatment is appropriate	You and your therapist decide what treatments are appropriate

THERAPY BUSINESS POLICIES AND PROCEDURES

Can we take a moment and do some breath work? Let's release the energy from all this money talk. Inhale for four . . . hold for four . . . exhale for four . . . hold for four . . . repeat however many times you need. Money is how we survive, and I want to be sensitive to your financial situations.

Okay . . . I'm ready to move forward, and if you are, let's talk practices and policies of a therapy business. First, paperwork ... ohhhh paperwork, so long and jargon heavy. If you're like me when filling out medical paperwork, you might just find the box where you sign and that's the end of reading the document. Even if you aren't like me, it's good to know that policies and procedures let you know what to expect from the therapy process. You can find this information in the paperwork you fill out before your first appointment.

COMMON FORMS *INDICATES A REQUIRED FORM	
Informed Consent*	Explains the risks, benefits, and outcomes of therapy. This form can also explain policies.
Policies and Procedures*	Covers things such as the no-show fee, the relationship with your therapist, how emergencies are handled, the social media policy, and the risks of therapy.
Financial Agreement*	An agreement you sign stating that you will pay co-pays, deductibles, etc. Also note that therapists are sometimes obligated to collect your co-pay. (The financial agreement may be combined with the Policies and Procedures form.)
HIPAA Acknowledgment*	Explains to you how the release of your information will be handled.
Release of Information	Allows your therapist to share information about you with another party.
Superbill	This is given to you if are self-pay and want to file it with your insurance for out-of-network benefits. (Used if your therapist is out of network or self-pay).
Telehealth Emergency	Provides an emergency contact for when therapy is performed over phone or video. Say you live alone and pass out during the call; this form allows the therapist to reach out to your emergency contact.
Insurance Authorization	Allows the therapist to release information to the insurance company and bill the insurance company.
Safe Harbor	If the client is a minor, this form explains to the parent or guardian when and how client information will be disclosed.

COMMON FORMS *INDICATES A REQUIRED FORM	
Intake*	The form that collects client data: symptoms, why you are seeking therapy, etc.

When looking for a therapist, it's also important to be aware of how the business itself operates. The therapist may be dope, but there may be red flags on the business side. Untimely invoices that are three to six months behind can be a red flag. Or invoices related to rejected claims that went unresolved. This affects the client because if the claims aren't resolved in a timely manner, the bill becomes the client's responsibility. Insurance companies have timely filing, which means therapists have to submit the claims for payment within a certain amount of time or the insurance company will not pay it.

Another red flag is high turnover of therapists within a practice. High turnover is disruptive for clients because they have to constantly start over with new therapists. Also, high turnover is a red flag for the company, because why aren't therapists staying?

Many private practices have a noncompete clause for clinicians. This means if the clinician leaves the practice, they cannot take their clients with them. If the therapist takes their clients, they are "competing." When the therapist leaves, sometimes the client stops going to therapy altogether. The problem with noncompete clauses is that they send a message to the client that what they want and need doesn't matter. Noncompetes are very common in therapy businesses. They are enforceable and, depending upon the state in which the therapy practice is located, therapists can be sued.

Mental health is not a competition. Many therapists have waiting lists. If anything, there aren't enough therapists available for clients. How can the care of people be of concern if a therapist cannot take their clients with them? When a private practice doesn't have a noncompete, it means the therapists take their clients with them if they leave the practice. This allows for you to continue your care and work with your therapist. My private practice doesn't have a noncompete because I want the therapists I work with to know that I value their growth in the field and I want clients to know that I value their autonomy in choosing a therapist.

A functional therapy practice will . . .

- Send bills or invoices regularly.

- Return calls or emails in a timely manner.

- Begin sessions on time.

- Allow therapists to continue seeing their clients if they leave the practice.

- Feel right. When you arrive at the therapy office, trust your gut from the first interaction with the person at the front desk to your session with the therapist.

Now that you are informed on how a therapy practice runs and operates, you are more equipped to make well-informed decisions about your mental health care. The reality is that as an operational business, therapy is not changing. But I hope this doesn't deter you from continuing your journey in healing.

You are in charge of determining what is valuable to you. Although I am a therapist who accepts insurance, I am also a client who pays self-pay. Both are equally valuable based on the person using said services. It is a choice. Even if you feel as if you don't have a choice, you do. Now may be a great time to dive into your Money Story and shuffle through what is important as it relates to your mental health. I'm not going to be that person to tell you to stop buying coffee to afford therapy because the truth is, coffee is important too.

DOPE TAKEAWAYS

» The value you place on therapy will determine how you prioritize it in your life.

» Paying for therapy with insurance means that you may have no out-of-pocket cost, a co-pay, coinsurance, or a deductible.

» An "in network" therapist is a therapist who accepts your insurance.

» Diagnosing is required for insurance but can be harmful when not done correctly or if you aren't well-informed about how diagnosing can affect you.

» Self-pay may be more expensive than using insurance, but it allows for autonomy in your therapy journey.

» You will be required to sign paperwork prior to your first session that outlines what to expect when starting the therapy process.

CHAPTER THREE

FINDING A DOPE THERAPIST

"There is no greater agony than bearing an untold story inside you."

—MAYA ANGELOU

inding a dope therapist is the most important step in your therapy journey. It may require some effort and patience. A dope therapist is a therapist you vibe with and trust. They are someone who has the qualifications to help you in your area of concern. You have made the choice to start your dope therapy journey—give yourself a big-a$$ hug! You may find your therapist right away, or it might be a vetting process. The process of finding a therapist can sometimes feel defeating. Guess what? You now have a dope therapist (me!) in your corner. I'm going to help guide you through this process by arming you with the right questions and information.

The therapist search often starts either online or through a referral. The task of trying to figure out if you and the therapist are a good match can feel overwhelming. When the search for a therapist starts, it's important to know what you are looking for in order to weed out the therapists that are not a good fit. Finding a therapist online is challenging because you're not sure if the vibe you get online will match the vibe you get in person or through video. Once you start the search process, you may not receive responses to your calls and emails or you may get the "sorry, I'm not taking new clients at this time" response. Most therapists will state whether or not they are accepting new clients on their profile, but some don't. There is nothing wrong with shooting your shot with a therapist who is full. If there is no response, it's the universe's way of narrowing down the search for you. If the therapist's profile states "accepting new clients" and they don't respond, continue searching.

To be able to provide dope therapy, therapists have a limited capacity for the number of clients they can carry on their caseload. For some therapists, this capacity may be determined by the number of hours they work or the number of clients they have. There are many factors that can affect the maximum capacity. Capacity boundaries protect you as the client. They are in place to ensure that therapy is a dope experience for all the clients on a therapist's caseload. This allows for the right balance of time, energy, and resources that are available to you.

Therapy is tricky. Although diagnosing works on a medical model, the diagnosis can be subjective. One therapist can see depression in a client, and another therapist may see bipolar disorder. There are some things to look for when it comes to deciding if a therapist is a good fit or if you should throw the whole therapist away.

One of the most common places to find a therapist is psychologytoday.com. However, there are many other resources outside of that site. If you are white and cisgender, locating a therapist on psychologytoday.com may be as easy as finding the wheat shapes in Lucky Charms cereal. If you are Black, Indigenous, gay, transgender, or belong to another minority community, finding the right therapist on psychologytoday.com can feel more like looking for the marshmallows. (If you ate Lucky Charms as a kid, you know how you felt when you poured the cereal and saw the number of marshmallows in your bowl—straight disappointment.) Although there are many challenges that may come up in the therapist search process, we are going to talk and try to overcome them. So, grab your water and breathing exercises. Let's find you a dope therapist.

THERAPY RESOURCES

When you're ready to look for a therapist, there are several resources available. You can . . .

- ▶ Ask a friend or someone you know who is in therapy for a referral.
- ▶ Contact your insurance company.
- ▶ Find out if your company offers an Employee Assistance Program (EAP).
- ▶ Search for "therapists near me."

Online resources include:

- ▶ Psychology Today (psychologytoday.com): the largest internet database of therapists

- ▶ BetterHelp (betterhelp.com): an online counseling platform

- ▶ Talkspace (talkspace.com): an online counseling platform

- ▶ Therapy for Black Girls (therapyforblackgirls.com): an online space dedicated to encouraging the mental wellness of Black women and girls

- ▶ Pride Counseling (pridecounseling.com): an online counseling platform with therapists who specialize in the LGBTQ+ community

UNDERSTANDING THERAPIST QUALIFICATIONS

You've started your search and you're thinking, "What the hell do all those letters behind their names mean?" The letters after a therapist's name let you know the type of education they have and what board provided their license. Knowing what the letters mean can be helpful in determining if the therapist is a good fit for you but not always necessary. In the United States, there are several main types of licensing boards for therapists with a master's degree: Family and Marriage Therapy, Social Work, and Behavioral Health/Mental Health. (Therapists with doctorate degrees have different licensing boards.) The exact names of the boards may differ from state to state, but all are in place to ensure that licensed therapists have met the state's qualifications and to give clients a place to file complaints about licensed therapists. The boards do the groundwork of vetting a therapist's education, work history, and background. They are there to make sure that those who use a licensed title have the knowledge to practice as a therapist.

Why are there so many different types of licensure? Trust me, even as a therapist, I find it confusing sometimes because it varies from state to state. A licensed therapist must have, at minimum, a master's degree. (The bachelor's degree doesn't matter as much. A therapist can have a bachelor's degree in TV broadcasting and then get a master's in educational psychology.) The master's degree matters because it's an emphasis on their foundation for providing therapy. For instance, a master's in family and marriage means the therapist's education emphasized interpersonal struggles and understanding couples and families. The education of someone who received a master's in school counseling, on the other hand, would have focused on providing mental health services in a school setting.

Then there are therapists who hold doctorates, the psychologists. Generally, a therapist with a doctorate degree has about five more years of schooling than a therapist with a master's degree. They can also perform psychological testing, such as the test for an attention deficit hyperactivity disorder (ADHD) diagnosis. The purpose of psychological testing is to gain a better understanding of your behaviors, strengths, and weaknesses, and to identify cognitive impairment. Can a master's level therapist diagnose ADHD? Yes, because there are criteria for it in the *Diagnostic and Statistical Manual of Mental Disorders,* Fifth Edition (commonly called the DSM-5), which is used for diagnosing. But a psychologist will be able to test for it. The difference is that a therapist is interpreting information from the client to make a diagnosis, whereas the psychologist is gathering data and testing for ADHD. A psychologist can diagnose and administer tests; a therapist with a master's can only diagnose.

Then there are the therapists who are in training and don't have a license. Therapists can practice therapy without being licensed, but they must either be in a master's program or have graduated with their degree. This is allowed when they are under the supervision of someone who is already licensed by the therapist's respective board. You may see that this type of therapist only has letters associated with their degree, usually an "MA" to indicate a master's degree, after their name (for example: Shani Tran MA, LPCC, LPC).

The name always comes first, followed by education (in this case, MA for master's), and then licensure. If the therapist has more than one license, there may be several sets of letters.

I am licensed in Minnesota and Arizona, which is why I have two: LPCC (Licensed Professional Clinical Counselor, in Minnesota) and LPC (Licensed Professional Counselor, in Arizona). When I was practicing therapy without my license, my name was listed as Shani Tran MA.

WHAT DO THOSE LETTERS MEAN?

The wording of licensure varies from state to state, as do the specific qualifications for the license. Here's a list of some of the more common licenses.

CMFT Certified Marriage and Family Therapist

LAC Licensed Associate Counselor

LADC Licensed Alcohol Drug Counselor

LAMFT Licensed Associate Marriage and Family Therapist

LASAC Licensed Associate Substance Abuse Counselor

LCMFT Licensed Clinical Marriage and Family Therapist

LCMHC Licensed Clinical Mental Health Counselor

LCPC Licensed Clinical Professional Counselor

LCSW Licensed Clinical Social Worker

LISAC Licensed Independent Substance Abuse Counselor

LMFT Licensed Marriage and Family Therapist

LMHC Licensed Mental Health Counselor

LMHP Licensed Mental Health Practitioner

LMSW Licensed Master Social Worker

LP Licensed Psychologist

LPCC Licensed Professional Clinical Counselor

LPC Licensed Professional Counselor

NCC National Certified Counselor

There are also specialties within the field. Therapists can specialize in working with a certain demographic, a particular diagnosis, or a certain modality of therapy, like Cognitive Behavioral Therapy. This can be helpful to know if you are someone struggling with, say, substance abuse or trauma and are in need of a specialized form of therapy. There are therapists who are trained to work specifically with substance abuse. When it comes to trauma and therapy, there are three types of therapists: 1) therapists who aren't familiar with trauma, 2) therapists who are trauma informed, and 3) therapists who are trauma trained. A therapist who is trauma informed knows what trauma looks like and may have the basics to start to explore trauma, but they are not trained in the tools and modalities required to heal trauma. A trauma-trained therapist recognizes trauma and can help you work through it, as they have the necessary training and skills. What if you find yourself talking about your childhood trauma and the therapist you have chosen has never worked with childhood trauma? A therapist who recognizes that your needs are out of their scope of practice is required to refer you. This doesn't mean you can't continue to work with your therapist. It just means that you would need to work with someone else for this particular concern. And yes, you can have two therapists.

You may have noticed that I didn't mention psychiatrists. That is because, although psychiatrists can do one-on-one therapy, they aren't known for it, and most don't. Most psychiatrists prescribe medications for mental health. For this reason, most of them require that their clients also see a therapist. But it's not rare to come across one that also does dope therapy. But don't take my word for it; let's talk to a prescribing professional.

DOPE EXPERT: DR. KOJO SARFO (@drkojosarfo)

Meet Dr. Kojo Sarfo, a dope Doctor of Nursing Practice (DNP). He specializes in prescription medications for mental health and ADHD. Because there is a misconception that psychiatrists and doctors only prescribe medication and don't provide therapy, I thought we would have a chat with him about why that is and what to expect when you go to see a professional who prescribes medications.

> **Okay, Dr. Kojo. What can we expect when going to see a psychiatrist, nurse practitioner, or doctor for psychiatric medications?**

When you go to a psychiatrist for the first time, they're going to ask you questions about your mental health history and your personal history. They are going to ask about your cognitive abilities and have you complete what is called a "mini mental exam," which will include questions like, "What is today's date?" and "Do you know who the president is?" They will also ask about your mood and ask about any suicidal or homicidal ideation as well as if you are having any hallucinations (if you hear or see anything that is not there). These questions allow the psychiatrist to have insight into your cognitive capabilities.

Sometimes it is necessary to do laboratory tests to rule out medical conditions, because thyroid conditions, diabetes, and things of that nature can look like depression.

> **Wow, I had no idea diabetes could look like depression! So, what should someone look for in choosing a psychiatrist?**

When choosing a psychiatrist, you should look for somebody with whom you feel comfortable. If you want to see somebody who shares the same color, race, or background as you, this is your discretion.

I would also recommend researching the psychiatrist and their philosophies before you go see them. If you go to somebody and they spend five to ten minutes with you and then prescribe medication, I would run away as fast as possible.

Y'all hear that? Dr. Kojo has given you permission to run if you don't vibe with the prescribing professional, so mark your exits. But what about people who fear the side effects of medications or worry that psychiatrists only want to get them in and out? What would you say to this?

A good psychiatrist will give you options for different medications along with their recommendation and explain any potential side effects. They will also answer any questions you may have. If you do not want to move forward with a medication, you can say so.

If the patient doesn't have a severe issue at that time, a good provider will normally give them the option of going with or without medication. And if the psychiatrist strongly believes that the patient needs the medication, they should be able to explain why they feel that way.

HOW TO FIND A THERAPIST

Finding a dope therapist can take some effort, but there are a few different avenues you can take. Let's look at some of those options.

USING INSURANCE

If you have insurance, you can call your insurance company to help you find a therapist. I spent some time working in the behavioral health department of an insurance company. In that role, I received calls from people looking for therapists in their area. When you call your insurance company, the person you speak to will ask if you are having thoughts of wanting to harm yourself or others; this is protocol. If you answer yes, they will attempt to transfer you to a licensed therapist because they are required to do so if you are actively having suicidal thoughts or urges. Insurance companies have licensed therapists available 24/7 to assist in crisis situations. If you answer no, they will gather your information to pull up your policy. Then they will ask questions to help narrow your search, like what your zip code is and what radius you would like them to search in. Then you can include criteria such as age, gender, race, religion, and LGBTQ+ to match your gender identity or sexual orientation.

When I worked for the insurance company, I would usually tell people to choose a maximum of three specifications but try to narrow down to the two that are most important. The more specific you are, the fewer options you will have on the list. You may not get all that you want in a therapist, but it is important to have one or two criteria met. Once the list is set, they will offer to send it through email. Ask to remain on the line until you receive the list; it limits having to call back if you don't receive the list. If you don't want to wait to receive the email from insurance, you can ask the representative to give you a few names, emails, and phone numbers over the phone. After you receive the list, I suggest heading to psychologytoday.com to see if the therapist has a profile there so that you can read a little more about their areas of specialization, their education, how they approach therapy, and to see what they look like. I mean, my last name is Tran and people have assumed I am Vietnamese, not knowing I got my last name from bae. Taking this extra step will save you from reaching out to therapists who may not be a good fit for you or aren't accepting new clients. From there, email three to four therapists on the list. Even if you have a favorite and are hoping to hear back from that person, *email more*. This empowers you to recognize your choices and still have therapists in the running if you get no response. A great way to go about this is to copy and paste the email you sent to one therapist and send that to the others on your list.

USING AN EAP

One of the most affordable ways to go to therapy is through an Employee Assistance Program (EAP). It's FREE! An EAP is a program that offers many benefits, including mental health services, to their employees for free. Through an EAP, you can usually have at least three free sessions with a licensed therapist per issue. Okay, okay, this program is so dope, and the reason why is because of the *per issue*. You broke up with your partner? Issue number 1. Feeling anxious about running into your ex-partner? Issue number 2. Your momma won't stop asking about the breakup, and you want to practice some boundaries? Issue number 3. You see how I did that? Give your HR department a call and ask if they have an EAP program. If they say yes, ask for the number. When you call the number that HR gives you, you will go through the same steps mentioned earlier to get a list of therapists from an insurance provider.

The EAP program is usually provided through an insurance company. Even if you don't have the company's insurance plan, you may still have access to the EAP. Most companies allow *all* employees access to this program, even if they work part-time. If you have the company's health insurance plan, you can still use your EAP benefits first. When vetting therapists for the EAP, you will want to check and make sure they also accept your insurance. There are several reasons for this. One, because the company you work for may not have the same insurance provider for the EAP as they do for their health insurance benefits. You're checking to see if the therapist is in network for both the EAP and your health insurance plan (if you have it through your employer). This will be helpful because you won't have to worry about switching to another therapist if you want to continue with your health insurance after using the EAP. An extra step may be necessary, and that is asking the therapist if they accept your EAP and your health insurance. This double clarifies, for added security, that you won't have to switch.

When you call your insurance or EAP, have the following on hand:

- Your policy number (for insurance; not needed for calling EAP)
- Specifications you want your therapist to fulfill
- The zip code you would like to use
- A radius for where you would like to search, such as 5 miles or 25 miles
- A pen and piece of paper in case you want a few names over the phone instead of via email

USING SOCIAL MEDIA

Some people prefer to search for a therapist in silence. Introvert energy come thru, I see you. Maybe you don't have the energy to talk, or maybe going to therapy is something you would like to keep private. That is where using social media can be your best friend. Therapists are plentiful on TikTok. You can search hashtags like #tiktoktherapist, #therapistsoftiktok, #counselor, #licensedtherapist, or #[insert your state]therapist, such as #mntherapist. Just like that, a plethora of professionals will come up. One of the cool things about finding your therapist on social media is that you get a look at who you will be interacting with before you show up to the appointment. Some therapists share their therapeutic approach, their education, and even offer tips on social media. You get an inside look at what it may be like to work with this therapist before you even meet them. If you want to get more specific, you can search hashtags like #substanceabusetherapist or #teentherapist. When you know what you are looking for in a therapist, put that in: #_____ therapist.

Remember to make sure the therapist is licensed in the state you live in. This may require a little more work on your end. For instance, if you go to my TikTok @theshaniproject and click the link in my bio, you will find that I am licensed in Arizona and Minnesota.

This means that in order to be my client, you would need to live in Arizona or Minnesota. You can then click on my website and see a *Psychology Today* logo at the top left corner. This means psychologytoday.com has already verified my credentials. I want to clarify this because I get asked a lot why I can't see people through video in other states. Even if you want to see the therapist via telehealth, you still must live in the state in which they are licensed. Therapists cannot practice outside of their licensed state. The only possible exception is if you start seeing the therapist in one state and then you move to another. For example, if you are living in Wisconsin and seeing a therapist who is licensed there and then you move to Arizona, the therapist would have to contact the Arizona board to see if there is continuity of care. Some boards do allow therapists to continue seeing their clients for a short time, until they find a new therapist in the new state.

But not every therapist has a website. If that is the case, you can look up the Board of Behavioral Health for the state in which they practice. Once you arrive at the board's website, look for a tab that says "license verification" or something regarding licensure lookup. If you can't find it, there should be a number for the board that you can call. Once you enter the therapist's first and last name, the system will let you know if their license is active. This is also helpful because you'll be able to see if the therapist has any violations against their license. If you don't see their name, don't be alarmed; it could mean that they are a therapist in training.

A therapist who is in training is required to be under supervision if they are doing therapy. The therapist is required to disclose this information to their clients. In addition, they are also obligated to provide you with their supervisor's information. When I say "supervisor," it is a little different than the supervisor we are used to in corporate America. First, the supervisor doesn't have to be onsite. Supervision just means that someone who has been licensed for a certain amount of time and is board approved will be helping the therapist in learning and practicing the delivery of therapy services.

Supervisors do this by looking at the therapist-in-training's notes and consulting with them about their clients. If you choose a therapist who is under supervision, your therapy notes are accessible to the supervisor. Information about this process is required to be laid out in the initial paperwork you sign before your first session.

USING CRITERIA TO FIND A THERAPIST

The therapy process is a vulnerable one that is easier to navigate when you find a therapist you vibe with. What that vibe looks like is up to you. One of the reasons I wanted a Black therapist when I was searching for services was because I didn't want to have to explain my Blackness. When George Floyd was murdered, my Black clients and I lived through those experiences together. There was an added layer and tone of "I get it" in our sessions. I knew what it was like to watch someone who looks like you or your father, brothers, and cousins die at the hands of white cops.

Even if you can't find a therapist who looks like you or shares your cultural values, it doesn't mean your therapist can't help you. What you are looking for is a therapist who has cultural humility. We are used to hearing the term cultural competency, which is different from cultural humility. Cultural competency means a therapist has the ability to understand, appreciate, and effectively interact with people from different cultures. Cultural humility is a therapist's lifelong engagement and commitment to recognizing their own cultural bias and employing frequent self-reflections to build an honest relationship with their client.

CULTURAL COMPETENCY	CULTURAL HUMILITY
May be developed through courses	Is developed through courses and working with other cultures and populations, and extends to the therapist's personal life

CULTURAL COMPETENCY	CULTURAL HUMILITY
May end after college	Is a lifelong process
Is helpful for the client	Is helpful for the therapist to self-reflect and build an honest relationship with the client
Decreases harm by gaining knowledge of other cultures	Increases awareness by developing communication skills to interact across different cultures
Promotes stereotyping and thinking of cultures as a monolith	Promotes differences across cultures
Uses whiteness and Westernized views as the norm	Uses differences in people to understand the person as a part of their culture

EVALUATING YOUR THERAPIST: THE INITIAL CONSULTATION

Before your first session, it may be helpful to ask for a consultation. This is a short conversation with the therapist, usually 10 to 15 minutes, and sometimes they are offered for free. It's time to vet the therapist. Now you may wonder, "How do I figure out if this is the best therapist for me?" There are a few questions to ask yourself when it comes to vetting your therapist. The first is, "What kind of person do I want to talk to?" I say "want" instead of "need" because sometimes we aren't able to identify our needs and it's easier to ask for what we want. For example, you may want someone who seems kind, warm, or professional; maybe you're looking for a motherly vibe; or maybe you want someone young, funny, or serious. Think about your own criteria. You can probably identify what kind of person you would click with from the beginning. Once you identify a list, look for these qualifications during the consultation call.

Another great question to ask yourself is, "What matters to you?" Maybe it's important that you receive therapy that incorporates your cultural beliefs.

> Yara is seeking therapy services after graduating from college. Yara is Black, female, and just graduated from her nursing program. She is struggling in her relationship due to cultural differences with her girlfriend, who is biracial. Yara has a passion for art and finds it to be a coping skill of hers. She wants to integrate art into her therapy sessions. When vetting her therapist, she asks during the consultation call if the therapist is familiar with art therapy. She also asks if the therapist is a part of the LGBTQ+ community.

Now I want to share questions you may not have thought about asking yourself, such as "What is the therapists schedule like?" Some therapists have an appointment-by-appointment schedule, while others prefer automatic rotating appointments. Or maybe your therapist only works mornings and no weekends. Will this type of scheduling work for you?

The initial consultation is also a good time to ask the therapist about their fees, even if you have insurance. Sometimes insurance lapses or doesn't cover all services. Maybe you are in need of an emotional support animal letter or you need your therapist to testify in court. Therapists can assist you in areas outside of the therapy session; therefore, it's important to know their fees as some aren't covered by insurance.

When contacting the therapists that you have chosen, it's important to ask questions that are related to the type of care you would like to receive. For example,

- Have you ever worked with anyone with [your specific concerns]?

- Have you ever worked with people who are similar to me in terms of [a specific factor, such as age, gender, or race]?

- How do you go about helping your clients resolve their issues?

POSITIVE QUALITIES

The following is a list of qualities you can find in a therapist. Go through the list and choose the top three qualities you would like in a therapist. Prioritize them and then ask: "Does the therapist I am seeing have these qualities?" Some qualities on this list may not be apparent right away but are important to keep in mind during the first few sessions with a new therapist.

Good listener

Validating

Encouraging

Able to lead the session

Makes therapy feel like a team effort

Reassuring

Specializes in my issue

Authentic

Flexible

Checks in periodically about the therapy process

Dependable

Responsible

Empathetic

Effectively communicates

Models healthy skills

Sets boundaries

Explains my diagnosis

Committed to me

Pays attention to therapy progress

Has cultural humility

Appears to know what they are doing

Is involved in continued training

Genuinely cares

Produces results

Understanding

Shows interest

Makes me feel safe

Builds trust

Supports the use of cannabis

It's important to remember that the therapy process is yours. The list that you created is based on your needs and wants. It is okay if you aren't sure what you want or need right now. If you fall into that category, it may be helpful to approach therapy with an open mind. Go to a few therapists, rank them, and then write down why you ranked them the way that you did. Finding a dope therapist is one of the most important parts of your therapy journey and can be the toughest. The therapist you choose will be the one guiding you. You want to make sure that, above all, you can trust and like this person because it is *you and them* on this journey, together.

RED FLAGS

During your search you may find some therapists who feel like a wrong Starbucks secret menu order. It just wasn't giving what it was supposed to give. It looked like a good idea, but the taste it left in your mouth didn't work for you. Just like we previously made a list about what can make someone a dope therapist, we also have a list of red flags—the things that make you say, "Yeah, Imma return this one."

Always cuts you off in session

You never feel better after your therapy sessions

You can tell they aren't paying attention to you

Consistently late

Doesn't give you the allotted time

Makes you feel judged

Imposes their views

Not sensitive

Breaks confidentiality

Initiates tough topics without asking

Doesn't define how they can help you

Has previous complaints with their licensure board

Attempts to have a sexual relationship with you

Talks about other clients with you

Shames you

Talks too much about themselves

Pushes you to talk when you aren't ready

Contacts you outside sessions in a personal way that is not related to your therapy

Gets defensive

HOW THERAPISTS DIFFER FROM OTHER PROVIDERS

There are differences among a psychiatrist, a psychologist, and a therapist. A psychiatrist is a medical doctor who can treat mental health conditions through the use of medications. Often the visits are short and rarely do you come across a psychiatrist who also does talk therapy. For this reason, in most cases it is recommended that you also see a therapist while on medication.

If you are on medication and seeing a therapist, it is important for your psychiatrist and therapist to communicate. You can allow this through a release of information. The therapist gets to be your advocate: a voice that speaks to your symptoms more in depth and relates them to the work you've been doing in therapy.

You may feel this is a breach of privacy or that your therapist may divulge too much. Know that you have control over what your therapist says. You can ask your therapist not to mention certain things. You can also decline that they communicate, but most clients find communication between their therapist and their psychiatrist to be beneficial. But at any point should you say, "Yeah, I'm good," you can revoke that release just as quickly as you signed it.

I have often found that when clients are feeling better or worse, they don't communicate with their psychiatrist. This may be due to any number of reasons, from being unable to get an appointment to feeling shame around mismanaging their medications. I find this to be a wonderful opportunity to step in and advocate for my clients. Of course, there is the piece of creating accountability, but sometimes it's nice to have someone in your corner.

It's not always a psychiatrist who prescribes medications; sometimes it can be your primary physician. This is awesome because you can usually get in to see them more quickly. As a therapist, I love communicating with primary physicians because I get an understanding of what is going on with the client medically. Information from your primary physician can help in holistic mental health care.

GROUP THERAPY

Because we are talking about finding a dope therapist, I want to take a moment to talk about group therapy. If you are considering group therapy, the vetting process applies to the group members as well.

In group therapy you don't get to choose who is a part of your therapy sessions. Group therapy is when more than one person joins a therapy session to be treated by the same therapist for the same issue, such as depression, grief, or substance abuse. When you join group therapy, it means other people are involved in your journey—not just you and your therapist. This may seem invasive and uncomfortable at first if you don't want people in your business. I get it. This can be especially challenging from a cultural perspective.

The purpose of group therapy is to establish commonality, but when different cultures come together in a group, it can sometimes have the opposite effect, making certain individuals feel even more isolated. Let's say you have a Black man who is experiencing depression and feels his depression is related to seeing Black men murdered by white cops in the news. He is a part of a men's depression group and the members are mainly white men. The Black man may not feel that it is a safe place to process and explore his issues around white cops. The Black man may feel safer and more comfortable in a group whose members mainly consist of people of color.

If you do find a group where you feel comfortable, it can be a helpful part of your therapy journey. Yes, you are telling your business to strangers, but there are some benefits to this. One of the benefits is that you don't feel alone in what you are struggling with because members are chosen for the group based on similar issues such as addiction, depression, LGBTQ+ concerns, or grief and loss. This means you can get support and validation from people who have the same concerns, which doesn't always happen in the individual therapy process.

One of the main reasons people attend therapy is related to dealing with interpersonal relationships. You may have heard the saying, "People often go to therapy to talk about people who don't go to therapy." In group therapy, you will learn how to use your voice and build healthy communication skills with other people. The group is led by a therapist who facilitates and assists the group through processing and interacting with each other. In individual therapy, you may learn the skills, but you won't always have an opportunity to test them; in group therapy, you can do both. Being challenged in group therapy allows for growth with the guidance of healthy modeling. With an excellent trained group therapist, members of the group will challenge each other to process, own, and become action oriented.

Are you that person who wants your therapist to tell you what to do? Therapists aren't meant to give advice; we are there to guide you to make choices on your own. In group therapy, you may get this advice. During my practicum, which is like an internship for therapists, I co-facilitated a depression group. One of the things I was amazed by was the advice the group members shared with each other. Advice ranged from how to deal with your family not understanding your mental illness to why attempting suicide isn't the answer. I find that people are more likely to listen when they feel not just understood but as though someone truly knows what it's like in their world.

Finally, it's worth noting that group therapy is usually cheaper than individual therapy—like, half the price cheaper. I know for some of you, finances play a huge role in whether or not you will go to therapy. A great place to start may be group therapy. And just like any other form of therapy, you get out of it what you put into it.

Did you know that you can do both individual therapy and group therapy? Check with your insurance provider to find out what your group therapy benefits are.

Finding a dope therapist may happen right away or it may take time. But know that there is a therapist out there for you. Armed and empowered with your wants and needs, the right questions, and an understanding of your choices, you can now confidently pursue a dope, healthy therapy relationship. We will talk about building on this relationship in the upcoming chapters.

PS I am proud of you. Now that you have found a dope therapist, it's time for your first session.

DOPE TAKEAWAYS

» Finding a dope therapist is about knowing what you want from the therapist.

» You can vet your potential therapist through their professional social media pages.

» Find two to three therapists to email or call, and contact all of them.

» Come up with a few questions to interview your therapist.

» Not every therapist is right for every client. Don't take it personally if a therapist declines to work with you. A good therapist knows their limitations and will try to connect you with someone who can help.

QUESTIONS TO ASK A POTENTIAL THERAPIST

Financial:

» What is your self-pay rate?

» Do you have a sliding-fee scale?

» Do you offer a payment plan?

» What is your policy around no shows/late cancellations?

» What if I get into a financial bind?

» What happens if my insurance doesn't cover the cost?

Training:

» How long have you been practicing therapy?

» What licenses do you hold?

» What demographics have you worked with?

» Are you familiar with [insert your concern]?

» What settings have you practiced in?

» What areas did you focus on during your training and education?

» What does cultural humility mean to you?

» How long have you been in supervision? (If the therapist is under supervision.)

» How long have you worked with individuals experiencing similar concerns?

» What interests you about therapy?

Therapist:

» What are your strengths and limitations?

» How do you approach therapy?

» What is your style of therapy?

» What tools do you primarily use and what can I expect from them?

» When conflict arises with the client, how do you address it?

» If we run into each other in public, what should I do?

» Why did you choose to become a therapist?

» What is your policy for contacting you in case of emergencies?

» What happens if you pass away?

» What happens if you are temporarily or permanently unable to continue working with me?

» How do you protect my privacy when writing your notes?

» What are your views on medication?

» What should I understand about mandated reporting, and how do you handle it?

Sessions:

» How often can I expect us to meet?

» How long are the sessions?

» Do you give homework?

» How should I prepare for our sessions together?

» How can I tell if therapy is working?

» How are therapy goals created?

» What happens if I don't like you as my therapist?

Adapted from @mydestanation by Dr. Desta, one of our Dope Experts.

CHAPTER FOUR

EXPECTATIONS AND THE FIRST SESSION

"You should never view your challenges as a disadvantage. Instead, it's important for you to understand that your experience facing and overcoming adversity is actually one of your biggest advantages."

— MICHELLE OBAMA

ou made it. You put in the work to find a therapist, made an appointment, and filled out the paperwork. Now the time has come for your first therapy session. I want you to take a moment and acknowledge how strong you are for choosing to prioritize yourself. Take a deep breath in through your nose for a count of four: one . . . two . . . three . . . four . . . and then let it all out through your mouth. Go ahead and hug the hell outta yourself. Healing starts now, but the work it took to get to this point should not be overlooked. I am so f*ckin' proud of you.

Meeting your therapist for the first time can bring on some nerves. Maybe you're not sure what to expect, or maybe you've had a horrible experience with therapy in the past and need it to work this time. Thank you for giving me the opportunity to guide you through your journey. As a therapist, I also get nervous because I know how high the stakes can be for the healing process. Sometimes everything is riding on therapy. The first session is an opportunity for you to see if a therapist is a good fit for you. To help ease some concerns you may have, let's dive into what you can expect from your first session.

WHAT TO EXPECT

If you are seeing a therapist in their clinic, you will enter it as you would a medical office. Some clinics are operated by only one therapist, which means that you may not see a front desk when you enter. If this is the case, you should find the therapist's office, and if the door is closed, wait nearby or in the waiting area if there is one. Once the therapist is ready, they will come out and get you. It's best not to knock as the therapist may be in a session with another client. There may even be an "in session" sign on the door.

If you are meeting a therapist through a video service, you will usually receive a link via email a few days to a couple of hours prior to your session. The link provided to you will guide you to a virtual waiting room. It's best to arrive a few minutes early to check your connection, audio, and video. You will also want to keep the therapist's email or phone number on hand in case you have any technical difficulties. It's okay if you don't see the therapist right at the start of your session; within two to three minutes, they should appear. If you've waited longer than five minutes, try reaching out to them.

The session usually starts off with a little small talk to help you get comfortable. During this phase, the therapist will go over policies and procedures. If you have any questions about therapy or about the therapist, this would be a great opportunity to ask them. I recommend that you ask your questions at the beginning of the session as you might forget them by the end. (See Chapter 3 for some great questions to ask.)

Because the purpose of the first session is to gather your history, you're going to be asked to provide a lot of information. Therapists often request information about what brought you to therapy, your current job and living situation, and symptoms you have been experiencing. The therapist might look away as you speak to take down notes of what you choose to share with them. However, all the information you give doesn't necessarily get put into your file. I can't speak for every therapist, but I leave out details like people's names, places, and other particulars to protect my clients.

The therapist is gathering all of this information in order to establish a starting point for your concerns and to compare them as you progress throughout therapy. What you say in the beginning can be considered a baseline to be used to determine if things are getting better or worse. For instance, you came in and told your therapist that you feel lonely and aren't sleeping. Over the course of therapy, your therapist will keep track of your sleeping habits and social interactions to assess for improvement.

During this information gathering, the therapist may ask you if you are having any thoughts of wanting to harm yourself or others. People can be hesitant in answering this question because there is a stigma that answering affirmatively leads to hospitalization. If you are feeling hesitant, it may benefit you to ask the therapist, "What is your protocol for suicidal ideation?" If you say that you are having suicidal thoughts, it is not grounds for a therapist to recommend hospitalization right away. A therapist should also check for intent (the likelihood of you dying by suicide) and plan (whether you have planned out how you will die by suicide). I say "should" because not all therapists handle suicidal ideation this way. It may be helpful to ask to assess your level of trust and comfort. Just having suicidal thoughts can be a normal part of what you are struggling with, and the information about your thoughts/ideations will be helpful in determining your treatment plan. (If you are having suicidal thoughts and you don't trust telling a therapist during the first session, please call the national suicide line at 800-273-8255.)

Your therapist may also ask about homicidal thoughts or thoughts that you want to harm someone else. I'm not referring to wanting to slap the shit outta your boss for his racist, sexist comment in the meeting. No, I am referring to active thoughts that you have the intention of causing harm to another person. If you divulge this information to a therapist, we take it seriously. Therapists are bound by the Tarasoff law and will have to report to the person that you want to harm. This is a law that requires all mental health professionals to protect people from bodily harm by a client. Basically, it's our duty to warn. This process may seem tricky to navigate because you may just be having thoughts and want to talk through them. Asking the therapist what their homicidal protocol is will help you understand. Your safety is our primary concern, and therefore protecting you from yourself or others is a part of our job.

Now we get to the good part, your overall concern. It's time to establish what you are coming to therapy for. The therapist will ask you questions about your concerns. If there is anything the therapist asks you that you aren't comfortable with, feel free to let them know. Rapport is being established, and it is normal if you don't want to jump right into certain topics. During this time, the therapist is also getting a sense of what you need from therapy. Along with what's not working, therapists are also interested in finding out what is working. When they find out what is working, they can mark those as strengths for you to use throughout the process. Therapists are also looking to assess whether your concerns are within their scope of practice. There are many different forms of therapy, and not all of them are helpful for all concerns.

TYPES OF THERAPY	WHAT IS IT?
Art Therapy	Integrates therapy with creative processes such as drawing, painting, and more to explore emotions and feelings
Acceptance and Commitment Therapy (ACT)	Focuses on accepting pain through mindfulness skills to improve behaviors and live the life you want to live
Client-Centered Therapy	A type of talk therapy that utilizes accepting you just as you are, regardless of what you say or do
Cognitive Behavioral Therapy (CBT)	Focuses on the connections among your thoughts, feelings, and behaviors to implement change
Dialectical Behavioral Therapy (DBT)	Helps to process and cope with emotions and teaches how to live in the moment
Existential Therapy	Focuses on you rather than your symptoms to bring attention to the choices you have over your life
Brief Interventions and Brief Therapy	Helps to reduce or stop substance abuse.
Eye Movement Desensitization and Reprocessing (EMDR)	A form of therapy for trauma to help with traumatic memories and relieve psychological stress

A therapist may be trained in a particular form of therapy in order to serve the needs of a specific demographic. Not all forms of therapy work with all the concerns that a client may want to address. To get a better understanding of this, ask your therapist about their approach or specialty and whether it would be helpful for you. This allows you to have a better understanding of how therapy with a particular therapist will work and impact you.

Mandated reporting should also be addressed during the first session. Many people aren't aware of what exactly a therapist is required to report, so it is important to understand how the process works before you proceed. Mandated reporting exists to protect those who cannot protect themselves. Certain issues fall into the domain of mandated reporting, including 1) sexual abuse to a child, elder, or other vulnerable person; 2) if a client mentions that they intend or plan to harm someone; and 3) if a client is a danger to themselves. Therapists vary in how they report. If a client starts to talk about something that may need to be reported, I make sure they are aware that they are entering a restrictive area. Once they enter, they can't go back, and we may have to change course from their original processing. In most cases, when a report has to be made, I inform the client and ask if they would like to be present. However, not all therapists operate from this perspective. Therefore, it's important to ask about how they handle mandated reporting.

Feeling drained like oranges at a Sunday brunch is normal after the first session. You may feel a variety of emotions afterward. A part of the therapy process is that it may feel worse before it gets better. This is because you will spend a bit of time explaining how you feel and why you feel the way that you do, and exploring different topics about yourself. Most people are not used to having in-depth conversations like this. There are parts of yourself that your brain and body have worked to protect over the years. And when these thoughts and feelings come to the surface, it can feel like the floodgates are opening, with no sandbags to slow the process. It can create feelings of alarm and uncertainty or of relief and ease.

ARE YOU COMPATIBLE?

Your first session is your time to figure out if you want to pursue this particular therapeutic relationship. Does this therapist get you? This is a notable opportunity to ask any questions you may have about the therapy process or therapist themselves to aid in determining compatibility. This may ease nerves, if you have them, by helping you understand what therapy with this therapist will be like.

The energy dynamic between you and the therapist is something you should pay close attention to. How does the therapist speak to you? How do they address your concerns? How do they respond when you ask questions? What are their facial expressions like while you are speaking? Does it feel like the therapist is listening? When the therapist responds, do you feel they want the best for you? What often brings people to therapy is the want for something better. Do you feel "better" is possible with this therapist?

Therapy is one of the few moments in your life where the stage is all yours. You get to be the main act! You want to have someone who is sitting in the audience of your show, rooting for you, validating you, supporting you, and challenging you. Validation from a therapist can show up in head nods or words. Support can look like not judging you for returning to your ex after y'all just broke up. Do you feel that you have an ally? We know that therapy is confidential, but do you feel you can trust this therapist? Do you trust that they are the one who can help you with your concerns?

You get to determine what compatibility feels like for you. It may take another two to three sessions to get into the flow. But, after the first session, it can be helpful to ask yourself what you liked and didn't like about the session. You may walk away feeling certain that the therapist is not the one for you, or you may feel that you found a therapist to start your dope therapy journey with. But there may be a few of you who feel unsure. If you are unsure, go easy on yourself. You may have to meet with the therapist a few times to feel out the vibe.

Just as you're determining if you and the therapist are compatible, the therapist is also doing the same. Don't be alarmed if a therapist refers you to another mental health professional. They could make this decision for several reasons. Maybe your concerns are out of their scope, or maybe they're already working with someone in your family. If you are struggling with an issue that the therapist doesn't feel comfortable addressing or has never worked with before, they are ethically required to refer you to another therapist. Therapists also cannot disclose who they work with, and sometimes working individually with people who are family members or friends can be complicated. As therapists, we hold your secrets, and we do not want to find ourselves in a situation where we inadvertently divulge those secrets.

Not every therapist and client will click personality-wise. Some people are okay with that and don't feel they need to like their therapist. Others require a personality vibe—this is up to you. How many times have you met someone who is great at their job but personality-wise, you're like, "Yeah, that's a hard pass for me." When I was looking for a therapist after I lost my dog, I thought I wanted someone who would tell me what to do and call me out on my shit. But turns out, I needed a therapist who was kind, soft-spoken, and specialized in grief.

You may think that mannerisms aren't important during therapy, but I think they are. The most common comments on my TikTok videos are people telling me how much they hate it when a therapist just sits there and nods. I admit I nod, but primarily to let my clients know I am still listening. In grad school, therapists are often taught to assure clients that we are listening without cutting them off. Nodding is a great way to show that we are still engaged in what you are saying.

I asked my dope community how they knew their therapist was the one, and these are some shared responses.

HOW DO YOU KNOW YOUR THERAPIST IS THE ONE?

I spend my session not in my head about how to fake answer or omit til time is up.

I feel understood, heard, and not invalidated.
And I feel hopeful.

I feel comfortable sharing hard things and look forward to going again.

I feel safe with them.

Helps me discover things about myself not by telling me but by guiding me

I don't feel the need to hide areas of myself in order to feel like they like me.

She started swearing when I did and I was like "hm you're alright"

She matches my weirdness. There is no pretense. She is not afraid to be her genuine self.

What matters to you when it comes to your therapist's personality? Even if you say, "I want a dope therapist," what does that mean? It may be helpful after your first session to jot down what you liked and disliked about the therapist. Then ask, "Why are my likes important, and can I deal with the dislikes?" I once had a therapist who just validated me, which felt nice in the beginning, but I realized that I wasn't growing and also needed to be challenged.

If you are someone who has prioritized the personality of a therapist, let the therapist know it's important that you spend time getting to know them. However, remember that not every therapist is okay with sharing information about themselves. Think of the first session as interviewing the personality of your therapist. Or maybe you don't want to know anything personal about your therapist and prefer to focus interactions on you. Awareness around your needs related to the therapist's personality allows you to build a more authentic therapeutic relationship.

OPENING UP AND BECOMING VULNERABLE

You're probably aware that in order for therapy to work, you will need to be vulnerable. But what does being vulnerable in the first session mean? It means taking a risk, sharing your innermost thoughts and feelings, and exposing your behaviors with someone you're not sure you entirely trust yet.

I want to say, "Trust me! Therapists are experts; you can just go in and give this vulnerability thing a try!" But that could be harmful to you. You don't have to be vulnerable because that's what you're supposed to do. Yes, the first session will require some level of vulnerability, but only as much as you're comfortable with.

The beginning stages of therapy are about building trust. Trust is built when you and your therapist work together. This comes from you trusting their expertise, trusting that they genuinely care about you, and trusting yourself. You could talk to the therapist about trust to explore what it looks like and how you both can be working toward it. According to Brené Brown, shame researcher and author of *Dare to Lead,* "We need to trust to be vulnerable, and we need to be vulnerable in order to build trust."

Throughout the therapeutic process, you and your therapist build trust in moments. These moments can be small or great. Brené Brown calls it the marble jar. As trust is built with your therapist, marbles are added to your jar. Say you tell your therapist something you've never told anyone before because you felt frightened and ashamed, but your therapist validated you. That's one marble. Your therapist validates your anxiety of being the only Black employee at a company. Another marble. Marbles can be added at any time. When these marbles begin to fill the jar, you will find yourself opening up and being vulnerable.

Therapists are trained experts in navigating and guiding you through the initial nerves of opening up. That's why we take the time to ensure that our offices feel comfortable. If you see a therapist in an office, you may notice that they have decorative items like salt lamps, diffusers, figurines, and artwork, and maybe a sound machine. The sound machine adds an extra level of confidentiality; it conceals your conversation from people passing by.

To establish comfort over video, also known as telehealth, the therapist may wear headphones. In addition, your therapist should be in a private area with the door closed, unless they reside alone. There are some situations that allow for therapy to take place outside. However, this must be communicated to you beforehand. Feel free to ask your therapist how they protect your privacy.

Even though therapists take measures to help ease you into vulnerability, it is yours to own. You get to choose how and when you want to be vulnerable. So, you have your first session coming up, and you're not sure how vulnerable you want to be. The first thing to do is breathe. I know that sounds very *duh,* but the truth is, we often forget to breathe when we are feeling our emotions deeply. That shit can literally take your breath away, and not in a good way. Take a deep breath right now: in through your nose and out through your mouth. Now that you've taken a moment, I want you to ask yourself: "What are my expectations of therapy?" We sometimes forget that we have preconceived notions about therapy that influence our thoughts and feelings. Now, write down those expectations. An example may be, "I expect my therapist will do a lot of nodding and ask me how I feel." Or, "I expect that the session will go by slowly, and I won't know what to say."

Now that you have your expectations, write down what you want to say in the session and how you hope to feel at the end. This allows you to see what you want to talk about and compare it to your expectations of the session. Sometimes a fear of being vulnerable comes from the uncertainty of not knowing where to begin and a concern that the therapist will judge your narratives. Take a look at what you have written down and write I TRUST MYSELF in capital letters. Yes, that's right—we got a little breath work and now a sprinkle of affirmation. Writing that you trust yourself tells your mind and body that you stand by their decisions and what they choose in the session. Trusting yourself isn't just about trusting that you can be vulnerable but also trusting that you will know when you are ready. Trusting that you will follow your gut if you feel uncomfortable or feel like the therapist or session isn't "right." Sometimes you can be prepared to bare your deepest struggles, only to find out the therapist you are meeting ain't the one.

DOPE EXERCISE: THE FIRST SESSION

Before the session

- *What are my expectations for the first session?*
- *What thoughts am I having about the first session?*
- *What do I want to talk about in the first session?*

After the session

Pay attention to how you feel immediately after ending your session. If you can, write it down. Try to identify two to three emotions from the emotions list in Chapter 1 to describe the first session.

- *Were my expectations of the first session met? Why or why not?*

- *What about the first session was comfortable or uncomfortable?*

- *How are my thoughts affecting how I am responding to the first session?*

- *Did we address what I wanted to talk about? Did I feel heard in the session?*

- *Was there anything the therapist said or did that I didn't like? If so, is this something that is a deal breaker for me?*

- *Is this therapist a good fit for me? Why or why not?*

It can be helpful to start off the session by letting your therapist know how you feel about being there. This allows you and your therapist to build rapport and to focus on the here and now. You'll be able to get a feel for the therapist's techniques and get a sense of whether they will be helpful to you from the get-go. This is also your first step toward advocating for yourself in the therapy room and asking for help. Knowing how you are feeling in the present allows your therapist to guide you and introduce relevant skills. You'll spend a lot of time talking about the past or the future in therapy. Implementing tools and skills during sessions allows you to process and get feedback right then and there.

FINDING YOUR WORDS

We know that therapy means discussing thoughts and feelings, but this is not something we are used to doing when we meet people for the first time. We are used to small talk. I'm here to ease your worry.

It's not your job to figure out how to start talking or to keep talking. This one is on us, the therapists. We got you. We are trained to get and keep you talking, even if you answer open-ended questions with "yes" or "no." It's all good, we can work with that.

But in case you are still wondering what to say, one of the most helpful things to do is to take a look at the intake paperwork you filled out. Usually there is a question on there that asks something along the lines of "What brings you to therapy?" Take a look at what you wrote and ask yourself, "Is this what I want to talk about in my first session, or has something happened recently that is more pressing for me to process?"

> Quinn, a 24-year-old, nonbinary Black person, is going to therapy for the first time. On the intake paperwork, Quinn writes that they are coming to therapy because they had heard a podcast discuss how important therapy is for Black people. However, Quinn experienced something at work the morning of their appointment. They are feeling less nervous because they had found a Black therapist; however, they aren't sure how to dive straight into what they want to talk about. When the therapist asks what brings Quinn to therapy, they respond, "I know I should talk to someone, ya know, trying to heal this generational trauma and shit. But white people at work got me fucked up asking me about my hair, trying to touch it and shit. On top of that, HR sent out a wack-ass email talkin' 'bout policies surrounding hair. Is it a coincidence the email went out after I got my hair loc'd? Hell, naw. But what Imma do?" The therapist not only validates Quinn's experiences but assists them in labeling their emotions.

If you don't know what to talk about, it's okay to let your therapist know that. If you struggle with communicating this with the therapist, they will usually recognize this in the session. Don't be alarmed if the therapist switches gears in the moment to help you communicate your needs. When this happens, it is our job to get you talking and to build trust. Sometimes I like to ask clients what they are interested in to find a common ground. Because I watch so much TV, I can usually find at least one show that a client watches that I watch, too, and build trust off of that. I like to ask about favorite characters or hated characters as it allows me to see what my clients connect with. Discussing shows can help the interaction feel more like a conversation, which decreases the power differential of the therapist-client relationship. We are building rapport without even thinking about it.

TALKING ABOUT MONEY

Your paper, a.k.a money, is hella important to discuss. We discussed money from a business standpoint in Chapter 2; now it's time to talk about having a conversation with your therapist directly about your financial situation.

In the beginning, it's hard to assess for how long therapy will last. For some, six months to several years of therapy can seem like a lot of money if you have a co-pay, coinsurance, or a deductible, or are self-pay. As much as we may want to live by the Ariana Grande quote, "I see it, I like it, I want it, I got it," it's not always easy to do so. I'm a huge fan of effective financial communication. Whenever I approach the topic of money with clients, I always try to be honest and upfront. As Brené Brown says, "Being unclear is unkind." A therapist who accepts insurance usually checks your benefits before the first session to be able to inform you of what to expect when paying for therapy. You may also want to know what happens if you can no longer afford the sessions. How will your therapist handle that?

Your therapist will likely discuss their policies for situations such as late cancellations and no-shows in the first session. These policies and any associated fees should be listed in the paperwork. (If you are like me, you skim through medical paperwork like you're scrolling past the terms and conditions of an Apple update.) While not every therapist charges a fee for late cancellations or no-shows, it is important to understand how those fees are incurred so they don't disrupt the therapy process. And lastly, insurance does not cover late cancellation or no-show fees. The last thing you want is to be surprised by an invoice when you're deep in trauma work.

WILL THERAPY ACTUALLY HELP?

You can be helped when you are ready to be helped. There is a therapist out there with the right personality and skill set to see you for you and help you get what you want out of therapy.

When it comes to getting help, try asking your therapist if they have worked with clients who have had similar issues. Ask them how they approached it. Maybe even ask what you can expect from working with them on this particular issue.

I want you to take a moment and acknowledge how strong and brave you are. You are taking the necessary steps to heal yourself and own your mental health. This is not to be glossed over. You are making yourself a priority. The first session can be scary and anxiety-provoking, but it can also be exciting, worth it, and cathartic. You can feel all of those feelings, and at the same time. As you go into your first session, remember, you got this.

DO'S FOR THE FIRST SESSION . . .

- Be kind to yourself. This a marathon, not a sprint.
- Be forthcoming about what you want from therapy.
- Be open to the process.
- Leave with a plan, such as homework, and what you can be working on before the next session.
- Give the therapist two to three sessions to assess if they're a good fit.
- Establish goals.

DOPE TAKEAWAYS

» Prepare for your first session by writing down your expectations of therapy and the emotions you're experiencing.

» Don't worry about what you're going to say in therapy. It's the therapist's job to lead the conversation.

» Expect to talk about finances in the first session. A good therapist will be transparent about cost and work with you to figure out an arrangement that fits your needs.

» Make sure you understand the therapist's policies and fees for late cancellations and no-shows.

» Not every therapist is right for every client. Don't take it personally if a therapist declines to work with you. A good therapist knows their limitations and will try to connect you with someone who can help.

CHAPTER FIVE

YOUR RELATIONSHIP WITH YOUR THERAPIST

"An argument can be made that relationship building is the treatment."

—LESTON HAVENS

The therapeutic relationship is so important that if it doesn't work, the therapy work is then interrupted. People have chosen to end therapy for reasons related to the relationship with their therapist. Maybe it was the way the therapist said something, the therapist's facial expressions, or even the therapist's techniques.

The therapeutic relationship requires trust, engagement, and communication throughout the therapy journey. When the therapeutic relationship is glossed over, it leads to increased dropout rates in therapy and unsuccessful therapy narratives. Sometimes a client has had a negative experience with a therapist in the past that taints how they feel about therapists and prevents them from seeking a new one. How do therapists and clients overcome the things that can hinder a therapeutic relationship, such as boundaries, conflict, or countertransference? We don't ignore it; we want to find a way to communicate effectively to address issues as they arise.

Countertransference is when a therapist has an internal reaction toward the client and projects their feelings onto the client. I have definitely made this mistake throughout my 15 years in the mental health field; some therapeutic relationships were able to sustain those mistakes, and some weren't. An example may be the therapist offering advice instead of remaining objective.

Just as there is countertransference, there is also *transference*, which comes from the client. This happens when the client directs their feelings about another person onto the therapist. Know that the objective of therapy is not to avoid transference but to instead become aware of it and use it in healthy ways to process therapy. What goes on in the therapy room is a good indicator of how you are in your personal life. You get to project and deflect with us because it is safe and healthy. Through transference there are opportunities to recognize your emotions as they surface, and work through them.

WHAT IS THE THERAPEUTIC RELATIONSHIP?

The therapeutic relationship is a close and consistent, healthy professional relationship between a therapist and their client(s) (if in group therapy), which involves working toward common goals to impact change within the client(s). You trust your therapist with your intimate thoughts, beliefs, and emotions. Should that trust be broken, you will more than likely end therapy or start to withdraw.

I often find that clients will talk around issues as trust is being built because they want to process the issue, but their shame and fear of judgment hinders important details. John Gottman, author of *The Relationship Cure,* states that trust is built in small moments. You are looking for reasons to trust your therapist but are also on alert for reasons to distrust. Navigating the world is scary, and without trust, we can find ourselves hurt both physically and emotionally. Once trust is built, your therapist can make it a point to circle back to the original story and have you retell the narrative, with trust established, to better process the emotions around it. Not all relationships are healthy, but the one with your therapist is supposed to be.

Together, you and your therapist can determine and align on goals for your treatment. The improved state of your mental health is a team effort, like Batman and Robin. You are Batman. You can stand alone, but you've found that having Robin (your therapist) there makes everything a little easier. The collaborative approach begins with you and your therapist agreeing to work toward the common goal of healing. Once this is established, you can work together to foster and nourish the relationship.

You may not be sure about the therapeutic relationship after the first session. This is common and understandable. The first session is used to gather information, which means it isn't always a great indicator of how your relationship will be with your therapist. This is also the only session where you may be asked to be forthcoming with information you don't want to talk about.

I encourage you to take note of your feelings toward your therapist in the first session, but leave room for the rapport to start in the second or even third session.

BOUNDARIES WITHIN THE THERAPEUTIC RELATIONSHIP

I once heard a quote that went something like, "The only people who don't like boundaries are those who benefit from you not having any." Ain't that the truth! Boundaries are important because they protect us. When people hear about boundaries, they often think it means not being *nice*. When, on the contrary, you are being very nice. To yourself.

A therapist's job includes making sure that the session wraps up and ends on time. Early in my career, I struggled to end therapy sessions, especially when a client was still processing. I didn't know how to wrap up the end of a session by placing a boundary around time. This led to me allowing clients to go over, and then cutting them off right at the top of the hour. Because I didn't have this boundary in place, I noticed some of my clients would doorknob confess. "Doorknob confessing" is when a client unloads something important at the end of the session when there's not enough time to process it.

This wasn't helpful for either my clients or for me. I would become anxious both physically and mentally toward the end of sessions. While having my own reactions, instead of attending to the client, I would be attending to myself internally. This was problematic as attention was being taken away from the client. This also left no time between appointments; I would immediately go from one client to the next. Irvin Yalom, author of *The Gift of Therapy,* states that the therapist has many clients, but the client only has one therapist. Not having a boundary around time left me rushed going into my next session, which was unfair to my next client. How can I ask my clients to show up authentically if I'm holding myself back?

I learned to tell clients what time the session will end during their first few appointments. I then wrap up the session ten minutes beforehand in order to process what was said in the session. This is a boundary that I am firm on unless there is a crisis. So much so that clients now internally regulate themselves to start to wrap up the session. They are able to tell when the session is coming to a close based on my questioning, and sometimes they even start to wrap it up themselves. My boundary prevents my clients from unloading, protects me from countertransference, and allows us to have an authentic therapeutic relationship.

As a client, having boundaries within the therapeutic relationship allows you to show up authentically and get the most out of your time with your therapist. A great way to recognize if a boundary is needed is by paying attention to your thoughts and feelings. Your thoughts and feelings will tell you when something is off and may need a boundary. Remember, setting boundaries is about being nice to yourself.

> Quinn has been waiting for their therapist to return from maternity leave, and when the therapist comes back, they are informed that their therapist's schedule will be changing. Quinn is relieved that their therapist is finally back, and they don't want to disrupt the therapist's new schedule. A few weeks into the new schedule, Quinn starts canceling. The therapist asks Quinn about the cancellations, and they say that the times don't work. Unbeknownst to the therapist, Quinn has been struggling to put a boundary around their schedule, which led to cancellations. They were afraid to say no to the times because they really vibed with their therapist and knew how hard it would be to find another Black therapist. Once the therapist is made aware of Quinn's scheduling boundaries, they are able to find a better time that works for both of their schedules.

Therapy is your journey. Even though the therapist is the expert, you are the expert on you. I can't stress this enough. You know when you are ready to change or talk about a topic. If your therapist asks about something you're not ready to discuss, this may be a great place to put a boundary.

How do you know if it's a boundary or if you are avoiding? Boundaries are different from avoidance. Avoidance is when people react impulsively, whereas boundaries are intentional responses from your awareness. Being aware of your needs and limits in therapy creates a safe place for you to process and explore.

CONFLICT WITHIN THE THERAPEUTIC RELATIONSHIP

What do you think about when I say the word "conflict"? Take a moment and choose an emotion from the emotions list at the end of Chapter 1 to identify how you feel. Most people are averse to conflict because of inductive reasoning—using patterns to arrive at a conclusion. You may remember a time when you were in the thick of conflict and it didn't go well; therefore, your inductive reasoning tells you that conflict is bad and something to be avoided. Boundaries, conflict, and negative emotions are present in every relationship, and the one with your therapist is not exempt.

A great deal of therapy work is appreciating conflict and embracing it. This is best modeled when conflict arises within the therapeutic relationship. From the therapist's point of view, conflict can look like a client consistently being late or not showing up, a client not paying their co-pay, a client cursing at them, or a client sending a friend request on Facebook. From a client's standpoint, conflict can look like the therapist not listening, the therapist running late, or the therapist asking them to make a change in their behavior that feels uncomfortable. Avoidance only increases conflict and exacerbates a decline in trust. By asking versus assuming, issues can be addressed to figure out 1) how we got here, and 2) where we go from here. This is the conflict approach. We approach the conflict and make no assumptions. When the client and therapist can process conflict between them, they can explore it, and explore healthy resolution skills in a way that can benefit the client in their personal life.

As a therapist, I have learned that it's often not conflict itself that people fear, it's the emotions that conflict evokes. Conflict, or disagreement, is a part of the human experience. Recall a time when you were in a disagreement, and think about the emotions that went along with that disagreement. The therapy process is about going beneath the surface and discovering the root and why. Some people have an imprint of conflict from their childhood that left behind emotions they don't like to feel. (I don't say "negative emotions" because all emotions are valid; they only become negative based on the output of actions.)

Conflicts within the therapeutic relationship can be an indicator of behavioral patterns. If something happens in the therapy room that causes conflict and goes unaddressed by you, it may be an indicator of how you address conflict in your personal life. The relationship with your therapist is a great tool for treatment. Approaching conflict within the therapy setting allows for a better understanding of yourself. Yes, therapists are to remain objective, but that doesn't mean that we don't fully and authentically invest ourselves into the relationship with you. Therapists want to help you solve things in a healthy way. Conflict, disagreements, or uncomfortable feelings are a part of life, so it makes sense that they show up in the therapy room with your therapist.

ADDRESSING CONFLICT

This is an opportunity for you to get immediate feedback and practice resolution in a safe place. Moving forward, let's reframe conflict to "conflict approach." I say conflict approach because we must approach the conflict before we can solve it. If we jump to solving it right away, without figuring out the how and why of it, we miss the purpose of therapy. Therapy is not just about solving things in your life. Most of it is processing, reflecting, clarifying, and gaining insight. If you can process the conflict, it will allow you to gain insight into the causes, clarify how you feel, and learn how to respond instead of reacting.

When conflict arises within an established therapeutic relationship, bring it up. Therapists welcome discussing your concerns. When bringing up the issue, be respectful. Cursing, name-calling, and outbursts toward your therapist are not okay and could put your therapist on the defense, causing them to prioritize protecting themselves over helping you process. That doesn't mean that you minimize your anger; there is usually a second emotion under anger. Be open to how your therapist will explore your feelings and thoughts around the conflict. How you feel is valid. However, the therapist may want to explore what led to those emotions in order to bring better understanding and insight to the situation. The conflict with your therapist is also considered a part of your work. Because of this, being open to restoring the relationship can be beneficial in learning conflict resolution skills.

Welcoming discussion of the conflict is your therapist's responsibility. Calm and validating responses from your therapist will help you achieve a resolution and restore the therapeutic relationship. Because the conflict is with your therapist, it is their responsibility to explain without being defensive. Your therapist should validate your emotions, as they are always valid. But remember that feelings are not always facts. Therefore, your therapist may challenge your thoughts about the situation. This will be helpful for you because many behaviors stem from our thoughts. And, as every relationship takes two, taking ownership of their role in what hurt you is also your therapist's responsibility. Therapy is about moving you forward in life; therefore, it is necessary to restore the relationship after a conflict.

When you and your therapist work to resolve a conflict between yourselves, it provides you with insight into how conflict can affect your personal relationships. Every client and therapist is an individual who has their way of relating to people, and because of that, conflict in the therapeutic relationship is not uncommon. Working through it in the here and now is one of the rarest tools a therapist can provide you. Now that you are armored with your responsibilities related to conflict within the relationship, the rest is on your therapist. Show up, approach conflict, and own the journey through the therapeutic relationship. You got this.

YOUR THERAPIST IS NOT YOUR FRIEND

Why can't I be friends with my therapist? *Sigh* This is probably the person you trust the most, in some cases even more than your bestie, so it would only seem right to want to be friends. There is a lot of confusion around why therapists and clients can't be friends. I get it; the relationship can mimic that of a friendship and the professionalism can sometimes get lost in translation.

TV and movies have a horrible way of showcasing the dynamic of the therapist-client relationship, from boundary-crossing Jean in the show *Gypsy* to Isaac Roa's countertransference in *How to Get Away with Murder* and the unethical friendship/romance between Camille and Klaus in *The Originals*. There is some understanding on the part of the viewer that this type of relationship is somewhat exaggerated; however, it blurs the lines between what is acceptable and what is unethical. The purpose of the therapeutic relationship is not for the therapist to receive something in return. It is a professional relationship where the sole purpose and benefit is for the client.

When you are building a relationship with your therapist, you come to trust them, and they become a companion on your journey. Let's look at it this way—imagine your therapist is your driving instructor. They support and teach you how to drive until you are able to drive on your own. Each lesson is meant to help you become a better driver. Once you learn how to drive, you stop meeting with the driving instructor. However, a friend is more of a companion who accompanies you to the destination and gets out of the car with you. This relationship with your friend is continuous, whereas the one with the driving instructor will end.

Why is it confusing, though? Because when we look at it from the client's perspective, therapists are like friends, and our relationship can be as intimate, or even more intimate, than a friendship. But therapists don't consider clients to be friends. You tell us about you, but we rarely tell you about us. Our trust is not based on quid pro quo. We have your back, but you don't need to worry about having ours.

Being friends with your therapist can blur professional boundaries and can be confusing for you. One of my favorite therapist characters portrayed on TV is Maggie from *A Million Little Things*. When one of her friends, Rome, decides that he needs therapy, she refers him to another therapist. As Rome's friend, it would have been unethical of Maggie to take him on as a client. Doing this could blur the lines of their friendship and would not allow Maggie to remain objective.

> Gemma, a 62-year-old Black woman, has been seeing her therapist, Gladys, for nine months. Gemma clicks with Gladys because she feels that Gladys understands her, especially since they are both around the same age. Shortly after the George Floyd murder, Gemma thought about protesting. With Gladys, she processed her guilt around never attending a protest as well as her fears of attending, such as being gassed, arrested, or injured. Then Gemma decides to protest over the weekend. She sees Gladys at the protest. Gemma thinks it is strange that Gladys doesn't wave at her, even though they make eye contact. At the next session, Gemma feels some sort of way because she thought that Gladys knew how big of a deal going to a protest meant to her. Gemma shows up to the next session and tries to

talk about how she is feeling proud of herself, but something is off. She recognizes she is holding back because she is really hurt by the fact that Gladys saw her but didn't say hi. Gladys notices Gemma is off, and, staying in the here and now, she asks Gemma if there is something bothering her. Gemma explains that she thought they were friends and doesn't understand why Gladys didn't wave or say hi to her at the protest. "I'm sorry that our interaction led to you feeling hurt. That was not my intention. I apologize for not explaining the therapeutic relationship more in depth. But you must initiate contact first in public, and yes, our relationship can at times feel like a friendship, but it is not," Gladys explains. Gemma leaves the session clearer about professional boundaries and the type of relationship she has with her therapist.

Therapy talk is different from friendship talk. Friends can struggle to remain unbiased and usually offer opinions, sometimes even clapbacks. When the conversation is therapeutic, it often involves your therapist encouraging autonomy in decision-making instead of offering opinions. Would you feel comfortable paying your friend $200 per hour to listen to you every time you talked to them? Why or why not? I'm going to make an assumption and say no, because we ain't friends if I have to pay you to hear me vent. You lean on them and they lean on you, for free. Friendships are about give and take. In the therapeutic relationship, you are doing most of the taking while your therapist remains on the giving end.

The most glorious reason that a therapist is not considered a friend is this: absolute confidentiality. We are *required* to keep your secrets. Friends are not. You can tell your therapist your most vulnerable thoughts, desires, and secrets, and they stay between you and the therapist. (Unless, of course, it falls under mandated reporting.)

If the conversation that we are having right now is hard to hear, let's stay here for a minute and not run from it. I want you to take a minute and ask yourself why you may be disappointed that your therapist is not your friend if that is how you are feeling? Your therapist is important to you. You may feel like your therapist is the only one in your life who truly understands you. And acknowledging that your therapist is not your friend means that the relationship will end at some point.

BUILDING THE THERAPEUTIC RELATIONSHIP

Every therapeutic relationship is different. Each client is a different person. So, even when two people have the same therapist, their individual therapeutic relationships will still look completely different.

Some clients like when I self-disclose when they ask me about my day; for others it's just a formality. I can tell based on their body language, their eagerness to interrupt, and how they ask. No therapeutic relationship is better than the other, as each is considered and measured based upon itself.

You and your therapist will work to find your rhythm. You may enjoy a little dark humor when you discuss your trauma. Others may want to know more about their therapist, like what they enjoy doing as a hobby or what their favorite food is. How the bond is built is up to you and your therapist.

As with any interpersonal relationship, effective communication is important. For therapy to work, being honest with your therapist is vital. You don't have to tell everything about yourself, but being forthcoming about details is key. When you leave out details, such as feelings and thoughts, you prevent yourself from being authentic to both the process and yourself. You may find that you want to explore a topic in therapy but struggle to divulge all the details. If this is happening, being open and honest about what you are struggling with can help you overcome what is holding you back.

I had just started seeing my therapist. We were on our second session. I felt anxious because I had a topic I wanted to explore, but I wasn't sure where to start. The elections had just taken place, and Arizona had flipped from red to blue. I wasn't sure where my therapist stood; who did she vote for? I felt that to truly trust her, I, as a Black woman in America, needed to know if she voted for Trump.

We were about 20 minutes into the session, and it just didn't feel right to me. Although I was talking out loud about my life, my thoughts were saying, "You can't trust her if she voted for Trump; ask her; ask her." Because I was still building trust with her, I was withholding information related to my Blackness to protect myself. This was a very personal question I would be asking, and frankly, I wasn't sure if I wanted to know because I really liked her and how she balanced me as a person; she was the Hufflepuff to a Slytherin. So I said to her, "I have a question I want to ask you, but I am not sure if I want to ask you. Can we process this?" We talked about how my thoughts were making me feel anxious AF.

We processed my thoughts about the question instead of discussing the actual question itself. She then said that I could ask the question when I was ready, and we could take it from there, processing if it needed answering and whether she felt comfortable answering. I asked the question and my therapist said, "I want you to be sure that you want to know the answer to the question and are okay with whatever the answer is. When you are ready, I will answer."

I left the session feeling even more anxious, because sometimes it gets worse before it gets better. I had to ask myself if I was ready to deal with the answer, whatever it would be. I decided there were three possibilities: 1) she voted for Trump; 2) she didn't vote for Trump; or 3) she didn't vote at all. On top of that, there was a possibility that I may need to start all over and find a new therapist if I didn't like the answer. F*ck! I decided I

needed to know because it would help establish a sense of
safety around my Blackness in therapy. I started the next session
off by saying, "Yes, I want to know the answer. Not knowing is
more harmful for me because I won't trust you and get what I
need and want out of therapy."

I communicated what I was struggling with when it came to building trust with my therapist. When you are honest about your thoughts and feelings in the sessions, you bring transparency to the relationship with your therapist. It provides an opportunity to reflect upon interpersonal skills, while sustaining the work of healing and leaving room for the therapy process to unfold in ways that are beneficial to you and allow you to better yourself. My therapist was willing to self-disclose and answer my question, which increased my trust in her. At that moment, she added a marble to my marble jar. Building trust in the therapeutic relationship allows for autonomy and authenticity. As the client, you can come to therapy as you are: beautiful in your struggles, eager to be healed, with a little mess in between.

Showing mutual respect is another important facet of the client–therapist relationship. When I get a text from a client that they want to cancel a session within the 24-hour cancellation policy, the messages almost always end with, "I am so sorry about the inconvenience; I understand there is a late cancellation fee." I appreciate this because they took the time to inform me. I find this to be an act of respect toward the therapeutic relationship to let me know they won't be able to make it and acknowledge the policy around late cancellations.

MUTUAL ENGAGEMENT

Mutual engagement is imperative in therapy sessions. This can look like you and your therapist being on the same page with goals. If you have one goal in mind and your therapist has another, you're working in opposite directions. Consistent check-ins around the goals of your therapy are helpful to address what is working and not working, and if you are feeling stuck. In moving toward the same goals, both you and your therapist are equally dedicated to the work. There may be some days where you do more talking and some days where your therapist spends a good chunk of time on psychoeducation. Not every session has an equal balance of work, but as long as there is a common end goal, mutual engagement will ebb and flow.

Through the boundaries, transference, and conflict approach, you are going to build a relationship with someone who will support the hell out of you. I find it a rewarding experience to show up for my clients and give them someone in their lives whom they may have never had. It's rare that we meet people on this earth who are willing to offer support and expect no emotional support in return, but that is the role of a therapist. Take advantage of the possibilities that can come from exploring professional intimacy where the sole benefactor is you.

YOU HAVE A HEALTHY RELATIONSHIP WITH YOUR THERAPIST WHEN . . .

- *You trust them.*
- *You don't hold back in the sessions.*
- *You feel you can show up and be yourself.*
- *You don't hold back on things that pertain to your culture.*

- *You are eager to meet with them.*
- *You feel safe with them.*
- *You are aware of your therapist's boundaries.*
- *You feel comfortable with the progress of therapy.*
- *You feel that you and your therapist are working toward the same goals.*
- *You feel heard.*
- *Your therapist encourages and empowers accountability.*
- *Your therapist provides support but is not your friend.*

DOPE TAKEAWAYS

» The therapeutic relationship is a close, consistent, and healthy relationship between therapist and client based on improving the client's life. Trust, communication, and respect help build the relationship.

» The strength of the therapeutic relationship is an indicator of the success of therapy.

» You and your therapist should address boundaries throughout the process.

» The relationship between the client and the therapist is not a friendship.

» Countertransference is when the therapist projects their feelings onto the client.

» Transference is when the client directs their feelings about another person toward the therapist.

» When something feels off with your therapist, communicate it.

CHAPTER SIX

INSIDE THE SESSION

"Life doesn't get easier or more forgiving, we get stronger and more resilient."

—STEVE MARABOLI, *LIFE, THE TRUTH, AND BEING FREE*

ost people are aware that going to therapy improves your life. However, just showing up to sessions isn't enough. In therapy, you will learn about your emotions, behaviors, and thoughts and how they impact you.

The most important aspect to remember is that you are always making progress, even though it might not feel like it sometimes. Choosing to show up session after session is progress. Every session may not feel productive, but every session is work. Showing up means that you are committing to both the dope therapy journey and to yourself.

You have done the hard work of finding a therapist who is a good fit for you and laid the foundation for your therapy work. Now it is time to work on the reason why you came to therapy. The processing you do in the therapy session is essential to you being able to implement change when you are not in the room with your therapist. This work involves you committing to yourself, knowing your Why, showing up, and using your therapist effectively. Doing all of these simultaneously is how you get results inside the session. But first you have to commit.

This comes before the outside work, which is what you do when not sitting in front of your therapist. The work in therapy is physical, behavioral, emotional, and mental. Why is doing the work important? Because learning how to cope with life is a skill that never goes unused. When you do the work, your life improves. Your symptoms get better; your behaviors come from a place of response; and you start living a life that is authentic to you.

COMMIT TO YOURSELF

Committing to yourself means prioritizing you and reevaluating certain aspects of your life to see what best serves you. We are used to placing others—friends, kids, family, coworkers—before ourselves. When you make the shift to prioritizing yourself and start reevaluating certain aspects of your life to see what best serves you,

you might feel like you are being selfish. But don't you matter too? To be a better friend, parent, employee, or child, you need to pour into yourself first. You need to take a close look at your needs and wants, and find ways to be able to meet them.

The world around you can change you in positive and negative ways. Checking in on yourself allows you to respond instead of react, which in turn allows you to pause, assess, and intentionally choose how you want to show up in the moment.

ESTABLISH YOUR WHY

Much of the work done inside therapy revolves around your Why. A therapist's job is to help you clarify, identify, and label what is happening so that you can gain further understanding into the causes. Instead of solving the problem, therapists are looking for insight into you. Why do you think the way that you do? Why do you behave the way that you do? And why do you feel the way that you feel? They want to understand how you came to be in order to help you paint the path to who you want to be. But your therapist can't give you the right tools if they don't know which ones to give. To know which ones to give, there must first be an understanding of your Why.

Your Why is different from your therapy goals. It is your reason for being in therapy and a part of how you see yourself in the future. If you went to therapy because you and your partner are arguing a lot, your Why may be becoming a happier person. From this Why, you might develop goals like arguing less, being assertive in how you feel, and setting boundaries, to name a few. To develop your Why, ask yourself: "Why am I in therapy?" "What am I looking to gain from therapy?" "How would I like therapy to impact me?"

Once you identify your Why, what will you need to change? You might stay in an uncomfortable situation because you know what to expect, even if the expectation is a negative outcome. Going through change can be challenging, but if you only talk in therapy and don't take action to implement what you processed, you may find yourself feeling stuck in therapy. Are you willing to change to achieve your Why?

SHOW UP

Part of committing to yourself is showing up to your sessions. Be ready to talk about what you are struggling with. Arrive on time, be honest, don't hold back, and allow yourself to sink into vulnerability. Being on time allows you to utilize all the time allocated for you, but this is only the beginning. Also bring your authentic self. When you come to sessions, you will unfold physically, mentally, and emotionally. You sad today? Come sad—don't say "fine" when asked how you are doing. You just got good news? Be excited—your therapist is excited for you too. Depression got you sleepy? Yawn—oh my gosh, please let that yawn out! The beautiful thing about the therapy space is that it's safe and acceptable to show up just as you are. I have had clients show up on video calls, in bed, room dark, with only the light from their phone shining in their face like it's a rap concert. When you show up authentic to your current mental health state, it gives your therapist feedback to better assist and guide you.

I know that most people see therapy as only talking, but when you find yourself in the space of not wanting to be honest, tell your therapist. Instead of faking through it, talk about why you don't want to be in the session.

HOW CAN YOU SHOW UP MENTALLY?

Showing up mentally means that you are prepared to process information within the therapy session. A lot of therapy is your therapist asking you questions to get you to think. When you are in the session, you allow yourself to safely go to those places where you think about the events that have impacted your life. You pause and search your brain for memories and words to create a narrative.

Mental work is clarifying. For instance, if I ask a client why they are angry with their boss and they say, "Because my boss gave me a bad review," I may follow up with, "What was it about the review that made you angry?" I'm looking to guide them into thinking more deeply about their emotions around receiving the review for processing. Is the anger about the review itself? Are they angry with themselves for getting a review of that nature? Or are they angry with the boss who gave the review? The client might say, "I didn't like the way my boss talked to me while giving the review." This mental work has encouraged the client to gain clarification and identify the cause of their emotions.

HOW CAN YOU SHOW UP EMOTIONALLY?

Now you may be thinking: "Aren't mentally and emotionally the same thing?" They are not. Showing up mentally refers to the thinking portion of the session; showing up emotionally involves you expressing how you feel. Yes, you may hear your therapist ask that stereotypical question, "How does that make you feel?" I like to think of the emotional part of showing up as identifying. Your therapist might ask this question because identifying how you felt about a certain situation provides insight into your behavioral response.

Showing up emotionally means identifying what you feel in the sessions. Say you are processing something your mom said to you over the weekend, and in the moment you aren't feeling the topic. You might respond by saying, "Talking about my mom is getting me angry." Or, if you are being emotionally charged by processing your promotion, you might say, "Discussing my promotion isn't making me as happy as I thought it would." Identifying what you feel relays feedback to your therapist to further assist and guide you into deeper processing or to pause to tend to your emotional needs in the moment.

Oh, and we can't forget about those thoughts that you have about what you are saying in the session. Say them. We often have two dialogues going on, the one we voice out loud and the one we think in our heads. Therapists also want to know about the one in your head. Be forthcoming about the emotions you are feeling. Remember, there is no such thing as a negative emotion; it's how you react to the emotion that can make it negative.

HOW CAN YOU SHOW UP PHYSICALLY?

Yes, a part of showing up physically is coming to the session. But there is another aspect that many people aren't aware of: allowing yourself to physically react to what is happening in the session. This part can be challenging because most of us have been taught to control our physical reactions as a form of societal politeness.

During my sessions, I often instruct clients to take deep breaths in through their nose and out through their mouth, just like we have done throughout the book. I find myself reminding them to open their mouths and let the breath out.

Showing up physically means listening to your body and what it wants to do. If the therapist is guiding you in a breathing exercise, attempt it. If you're holding back tears, let them out. Now, as I talk about physically showing up, I want to remind you that this part may require unlearning some societal norms. Maybe you've been told that yelling isn't appropriate or that not making eye contact when someone talks to you is a sign that you're not listening. In therapy, you get to explore away from societal norms. As long as you are not harming the therapist or yourself, let that emotionally charged energy flow through physical movement.

Whenever you choose to go to therapy, try blocking out at least 15 minutes before and 15 minutes after each session. Too often, we rush from one activity to the next, never truly giving each activity our full selves. Studies have shown that it takes the average person

15 to 20 minutes to get out of the headspace they were in before they can properly move on to the next task. That 15 minutes beforehand will allow you to settle into your therapy mind and think about how you would like to use the session. The 15 minutes after will allow you to process and wind down from the session.

Now you can put all this together to show up mentally, emotionally, and physically (a.k.a. authentically) to your next session.

OWN IT

The beginning stages of healing allow room for your emotions as you process what has happened to you. But eventually, you have to move from victim mode to survivor mode, and a part of that process is owning it. Now, owning it can be done in many different ways. It could be taking responsibility for the role you played in a relationship coming to an end. Or it could be taking control over your narrative after a traumatic event. And it's probably not continuing to follow your ex on social media after they did you dirty.

When you take control of your healing experience, you take control over your narrative and life. I look at ownership as energy. That energy you are giving to wishing things hadn't happened to you could be used to accept things the way they are. This is called radical acceptance. You are not agreeing or condoning the situation, but you are acknowledging that it happened or exists. Owning that the situation exists allows you to take appropriate action to change it. An example of radical acceptance would be changing, "This isn't fair that I have to heal after my partner dumped me" to "My partner broke up with me (acknowledging and accepting), and I am healing through therapy (the appropriate action you chose to take)." That energy used to hate your ex could be used to love you.

DOPE EXERCISE: OWN YOUR HEALING

Take accountability for your actions and own that sometimes what you are doing can be more harmful than helpful. As a matter of fact, have you gotten a therapy journal yet? If so, let's do some journaling. Go ahead and grab it. In my Katt Williams voice, "I'll wait . . ."

- *Write down what you are trying to heal from.*

- *Write down the things you are doing that are helping you heal.*

- *Write down the things you are doing that are harmful to your healing.*

- *Now compare the two lists and ask yourself, "What do I need to own or take accountability for?"*

When you look at this list, what do you feel? Now would be a good time to reference the list of emotions at the end of Chapter 1. Label all them emotions, coz they is present and talking to you. Ask yourself: "What are my emotions telling me?"

> My best friend of 15 years ghosted me in July 2018. I spent the next few months frantically trying to reach out to him, texting him back-to-back, and leaving disgruntled voicemails. I then spent the next year in therapy, processing the hurt and betrayal. When the ball dropped on New Year's Eve, it came with tears and anger because I was starting a new year without my best friend. I remember coming home from the bar, lying on the floor, and debating whether or not I should text him happy new year. The tears started to roll down my face because I knew I still had hope for our friendship, and the reality of not accepting that the friendship had ended sank in. I was deep in my emotions, not practicing radical acceptance, which led to text trigger fingers. Instead of asking myself what my emotions were telling me,

I decided to text him. Right after I hit send, I rolled over and cried the hard cry that makes you ball up and choke; the kinda cry that you feel viscerally. I so badly wanted my best friend back, but in reality, I had no control over it. My behavior of continuing to reach out to him was doing me more harm than good because every time I would text him, I would constantly and anxiously check my phone to see if he replied. And then when he hadn't replied, I would feel frustrated and angry. That New Year's I told myself that if there was no response when I woke up in the morning, I would never reach out to him again. That was a f*cking lie, and I knew it. I went on to text him several more times throughout the year, feeling more and more hurt each time he didn't respond.

Had I listened to what my emotions were telling me, I would have heard them screaming, "YOU ARE HURTING AND IN NEED OF COMFORT!" Sending him text messages was not comforting; instead, it exacerbated my pain, and I was reliving the betrayal all over again. I was hanging on to the idea that he may eventually change his mind about ghosting and respond to me. I wasn't owning that I needed to focus on my needs and wants around healing.

I eventually did take responsibility and own my healing. Healing involved me not texting him when I felt emotional and instead journaling what I would like to text him. Do I still think about him? F*ck yeah, but it doesn't hurt as much as it used to. Instead of texting him every time I think of him, I say to myself in a whisper, "I'm thinking about you, and I am grateful for the 15 years of friendship." This comforts me because instead of only focusing on the hurt, I give gratitude some airtime. My text trigger fingers are less reactive to my thoughts when I think of him that way. This is helpful to me because I have accepted that he is no longer in my life, which allows me to control my actions and healing. I don't know why he ghosted me. I probably never will, and that's okay. He served his purpose in my life, and I am grateful for our time as friends.

Healing is my responsibility and I had to own that. What aren't you owning about your healing?

WHY DO YOU HOLD BACK IN THERAPY SESSIONS?

I didn't think it was the right time to give that information. I have big trust issues.

Shame and embarassment until I learned that things were out of my control as a child.

Fear of dissociating/ having a panic attack/ spiraling after session. Shame.

My story wasn't validated.

Afraid of judgment. That she would see me in the negative way I see myself.

I didn't feel safe. Lifelong trauma taught me not to speak.

Knowing how to give constructive feedback to a therapist wasn't taught to me.

I wasn't ready to confront and hold myself accountable for certain actions.

DON'T HOLD BACK

You will only get as far as you are willing to allow your therapist to guide you. You *have* to talk in therapy. It is that simple, and it's not that simple. Because in the process of therapy, you have what you are saying and what you're thinking. In order to get something out of this healing process, you're gonna have to talk and talk about what you are thinking.

Yara has been seeing her therapist for over a year. After getting into a pattern of verbal arguments and fistfights, Yara and her girlfriend Laila have broken up. Yara has been learning more about her anxious attachment style in therapy. Yara felt left out whenever Laila would go out for a girls' night and often sought intimacy with Laila through protest behaviors. Yara and her therapist processed the breakup extensively in her therapy sessions, and Yara reported feeling like she had moved on.

One night, Yara sees Laila out at a bar, gets drunk, and ends up sleeping with her. During her next therapy session, Yara holds back from her therapist. She leaves out the details of her encounter with Laila because she feels ashamed about going back to her ex after making so much progress in therapy. When her therapist asks how she's doing, Yara avoids the topic and says, "Good." Her therapist can tell Yara is holding back based on the lack of detail in her narrative around her weekend festivities, her shift in body weight, and her lack of eye contact compared to previous sessions. Yara reports that she did run into Laila but holds back on the intimate encounter. At the end of the session, Yara and her therapist discuss how boundaries would continue to help her heal. Yara feels ready to implement boundaries around Laila because she finds it difficult to ignore Laila's calls and continues to follow her on social media. Thinking about the encounter in session makes Yara feel overwhelmingly angry, and she ends up sending Laila text messages calling her names and cussing her out after the session ends. Yara is tired of the cycle. However, because Yara held back information about her recent encounter with Laila, her therapist isn't aware of all the areas of Yara's life that could use boundaries when it comes to Laila.

A few sessions later, when Yara expresses that the boundaries aren't working, she and her therapist have to backpedal. Somewhere along the line, Yara felt the need to hold back. She was ashamed of how her therapist would see her. Her therapist spends time inquiring about when Yara started to feel that way. After addressing the trust within the therapeutic relationship, they spend the next few sessions revisiting the original story of running into Laila. The two of them learn that Yara's shame often leaves her feeling guilty, especially because her therapist had said she was proud of the work Yara was doing. Yara feels that she has deceived her therapist. She works through holding back and processes why she didn't feel comfortable divulging running into Laila and how it hindered her authenticity and growth within the sessions.

Talking about what you are thinking can be hard. Shortly after having my second child, my therapist once asked me to identify how I felt about my husband's contribution to our household tasks. I said that I felt overwhelmed, but what I was thinking was, "It's not fair that he gets to just provide and society tells him that's okay and enough." Although I identified my emotions, I was actually holding back on the thoughts that could have helped me process how I *truly* felt about the situation.

Some days you may not know what to say. Other days you may enter the session feeling like there's not enough time for what you have to say or that you aren't ready to talk. And then there are the days where you feel like you talk too much. First off, you can *never* talk too much in therapy. Clients sometimes say, "I feel like I'm rambling." Rambling is just the expression of the unprocessed emotions and thoughts you have pent up inside you. They need to be released. Not knowing what to say is also normal. Those 15 minutes before the session is an opportunity to plan how you want to use your session. And then, if you know what you want to process but don't feel ready to talk about it, you can spend the session talking about why you feel you aren't ready.

~~~~~~

DOPE EXPERT: COURTNEY TRACY, LCSW, PSYD (@the.truth.doctor)

You may still be wondering, "But how do I not hold back? How do I just walk into the session and cathartically let loose?" I want to bring in Dr. Courtney Tracy, a.k.a. The Truth Doctor. Not only is she a dope therapist, but she has faced her own struggles with substance abuse and borderline personality disorder.

Courtney, can you help us understand why it is important to not hold back in therapy?

The world has taught you to hold back. It's taught you to assume you're wrong and that you need to conform and listen more than speak. This is the purpose of therapy: to teach you how to be free *and* how to respond to the real world when it's upset at you for not holding back. If you've got the right therapist, you're bound to learn the right skills and realize your right to freedom.

You have this theory on testing your fear line. What does this look like in a therapy session?

Testing your fear line in therapy looks like you showing up bare-faced, wearing sweat pants, and in tears, when you otherwise look like Beyoncé in public. It looks like saying something you're afraid to say anywhere else. It looks like practicing saying things while pretending that another person is sitting in front of you (a.k.a. the empty chair technique) and learning how your body responds so that you can become comfortable doing things you're scared to do outside of the therapy office. Testing your fear line in therapy looks like baby steps, like dipping your toe into the pool of your resistance.

~~~~~~

If I am hearing Dr. Courtney correctly, she is saying, make the choice to let therapy be the space where you are free. Not holding back means that you choose freedom. It means that you leave the outside world behind when you enter the therapy space. But she doesn't stop there; she gives a clear direction to being forthcoming, and that is by testing your fear line, which is a potential reason that people hold back in therapy.

You can be forthcoming in therapy because it's a part of you. Not holding back is the part of you that's raw and may only show when others aren't around. But in order to get more comfortable sharing this part of yourself in front of others, you need to practice. When you practice in a safe environment such as therapy, you can learn more about how your body responds to being uncomfortable to become more comfortable. (Kind of like that saying, "You have to get comfortable with being uncomfortable.") You don't have to dive into the deep end, unless of course you want to. Small steps are okay. You get to decide the pace. Me personally, I like to slowly get into the pool and adjust to the water temperature.

If you are still struggling with holding back in therapy, ask your therapist if there is something that you can be doing physically that occupies you while you talk. Maybe ask them if they have any therapy games or puzzles. This works well to get you out of your head and bring you into the present moment in the session. When you do this, you allow yourself to be more forthcoming by focusing on an activity that relaxes your nervous system.

The nervous system is the center for activities such as thinking, learning, and memory. There are three major tasks for this system to perform: 1) to interpret information from the environment and inside the body, 2) to interpret the information it receives, and 3) to respond to that information. Basically, it helps the body communicate. When the nervous system is relaxed, it activates the parasympathetic nervous system. The parasympathetic nervous system slows your stress response and calms your mind and body. Essentially you get your body to feel safe, which allows you to open up more in the session.

INVITE YOUR LOVED ONES INTO THERAPY

Sometimes it's helpful to have family members or friends come to your sessions. If you spend a great deal of time talking about your partner in therapy, you may find it beneficial to have them join you in a session. Some clients like this idea because it's an opportunity to practice the tools and skills they are learning in therapy, such as effective communication. This is also an opportunity to jointly problem-solve their concerns with their partner. However, other clients may be opposed because they don't want to share their therapy space with their partners or may not be ready for this next phase.

More often than not, clients respond positively to having people in their lives join in their therapy sessions. Even if the session doesn't meet your expectations, it's an opportunity to gain deeper understanding of your relationship with another person, whether that's a friend, family member, child, parent, or partner. You could come out of it with a new way of viewing problems with people in your life. Or you could get a better sense of things that you and the person in your life may not see.

How can you utilize having a loved one join your therapy session? The first thing is to understand that in this context, "loved one" refers to any individual in your life whom you are struggling with interpersonally and whose concerns you would like to understand. Once you have established that you would like to have them join, talk to your therapist about this. When talking to your therapist, address any concerns you have about the person joining, what you hope to gain from the joint session, what you don't want to talk about with the person in the session, and the purpose of having them in the session. This will help your therapist guide the session. Know that it may be a few sessions before the person joins after you bring it up to your therapist. This will allow you and your therapist to come up with a game plan to help you get the most out of the joint session.

There are several ways that you can utilize the opportunity of a joint session. Be open to hearing what the other person has to say about the concerns. This allows the therapist to get information so that they can help guide problem-solving within the session. It is also helpful because it will clarify how the other person perceives the concerns. Now that you have heard what they have to say, respond with "I" statements. Say you invited your mom to the session and she says that she feels that y'all argue because you never listen. An "I" statement response to your mom may look something like, "I feel blamed for our arguments, which upsets me." Two things happen when you use "I" statements: 1) you take accountability for your feelings; and 2) you effectively communicate how you are feeling. "I" statements are just one of the few ways to practice effective communication.

To practice effective communication is to have an open mind, listen, identify your emotions, know the intention of the conversation, and be conscious of your tone of voice. You still convey the information to the other person, but in a way that gets to the root with the intention of being heard and hearing the other person.

USE YOUR THERAPIST

You are the expert on your life, and your therapist is the expert on finding the right skills and tools to equip you with to manage your concerns. Use your therapist to get what you need out of them.

What happens in the therapy room is a small, yet large, moving part of your life. How you show up in the world will manifest itself in the therapy session, even if you try to hide it.

Use you therapist to test your theories and let your thoughts roll. What you say is confidential. (Unless, of course, it falls under mandated reporting.) And if your therapist has made you feel judged for your thoughts and behaviors, fuck 'em. That's a sign that it may be time to find a new therapist.

If you're trying to figure out how to address something with a person in your life, tell your therapist. You can role-play with your therapist to create authenticity around responses and feelings. If your therapist conceptualizes your thoughts incorrectly or says something you don't like, please, please tell them.

> In one of his sessions, George has a moment where he cries uncontrollably because he has just found out that his partner is leaving him. His therapist asks what he needs, and George says, "Do you honestly care?" "George, I care more about you than I think you know," his therapist says, employing the here and now. "The f*ck is that supposed to mean?" he responds. "Am I upsetting you?" responds the therapist empathetically. "Yes, because you're always so nice to me. No one actually treats me like you do, and it's frustrating because it's your job and you don't actually care." "Ouch, it hurts hearing you say I don't care," reflects the therapist. "Oh, I'm not trying to hurt your feelings," George quickly responds. His therapist interjects, "George, it's okay that my feelings are hurt, and I think you are hurt, too, right now because what you need from me is outside of our therapeutic relationship. Because I can't meet you there, you want to push me away." George thinks for a second and says, "Well, everyone eventually leaves, so I figure why not force you to leave."

If his therapist had avoided using the here and now with George, George wouldn't have been able to use his therapist to process how he feels about people in his life. His loneliness is apparent, and using the here and now helped him recognize why he pushes people away. Use your therapist; we can handle it!

YOUR DIAGNOSIS DOES NOT DEFINE YOU

Part of doing the work in the session is to not let your diagnosis define you. You are a whole-a$$ person outside your diagnosis. If you are someone who feels defined by your diagnosis, then part of the work in the therapy session is about breaking down those barriers. Because this is a dope therapy journey, and therapy is about figuring out who you are, not what you are.

Let's bring back Dr. Courtney Tracy one last time for her insight on diagnosing. She has struggled personally with diagnosing due to the stigma attached to borderline personality disorder diagnoses.

~~~~~~

DOPE EXPERT: COURTNEY TRACY, LCSW, PSYD
(@the.truth.doctor)

> **You can relate to the stigma of diagnosing. What are some tips for people when they feel that their diagnosis defines them?**

A diagnosis is a word. A word made up to categorize certain symptoms. Those symptoms are not the only thing you currently experience, have experienced, or will experience in your life. My first tip is to try not to focus on the word. It's limiting; that's why it feels that way. You have a name. That is who YOU are. And your symptoms have a name. That is what THEY are. You are not your diagnosis. My second tip is to realize that with this word comes a community of other people whose symptoms have the same categorization. This means you're not alone, and that there are people who are working hard to help you and your community find solutions and relief from your symptoms. And lastly, my third tip is that it's okay to feel lost at first. Allow yourself to feel the feelings of discomfort around a new diagnosis. There's a message there, and even if we don't want to hold on to it for too long, we need to know what it means and why we're feeling it.

~~~~~~

Even Dr. Courtney agrees with listening to what your feelings are telling you. Now that you are aware of how to effectively utilize your time in your therapy sessions, be open to what can take place during that process. When you start the therapy journey, you may not know what to expect. Every session is open to new possibilities. I wish I could tell you how your journey will turn out, but I can't because there are so many possibilities. There is no map because your journey is yours, and nobody else's. You get to create the map. My question for you is: How can you show up differently inside the session to attain your therapy goals realistically and stay true to your Why?

DOPE TAKEAWAYS

» Show up to your appointments mentally, emotionally, and physically, embracing who you are in the moment.

» Own your thoughts, feelings, and behaviors to get more out of therapy.

» Don't hold back.

» If you are struggling to get talking, ask your therapist if there are activities that you can do while talking.

» Inviting people into your sessions may be helpful.

» Use your therapist.

CHAPTER SEVEN

OUTSIDE THE SESSION

*"Recognize the ego for what it is: a collective dysfunction,
the insanity of the human mind."*

—ECKHART TOLLE, *A NEW EARTH*

common misconception is that most change takes place inside the therapy sessions. This is true to a certain extent. Changes in your thoughts and emotions can take place inside the therapy session. But behavioral changes—what most people are seeking in order to improve their lives—take place when you internalize what you learned from inside the therapy session and apply it to your life. To be able to grow from therapy and implement change in your life, you must extend therapy beyond the session.

But how do you take what you learned from your therapy sessions and apply it to your life? You practice the skills and tools you learned in therapy. The first step is reflecting on what you process with your therapist to identify where action is needed. For example, if you talked about setting boundaries with your therapist, practice setting a boundary prior to your next appointment. You have already committed to the process; therefore, I assume that you are ready to put in the work to create change. The work needs to happen in order to become the person you want to be when therapy ends.

The success of therapy is up to you. You may want therapy to be successful, and want it really f*ckin bad, but remember that doing is the gray area between wanting and getting. It's like saying, "I want to stop scrolling social media before bed." This is the want. The do is when you make an effort to set a timer and put your phone away before bed. How bad do you want it? Are you willing to take accountability and complete action steps?

The tough part about change is implementing it. We often know things need to change when we aren't getting the results we want. But even when we know change must happen, we fear it. Instead of embracing it, we step back from it, even though it's offering us a better outcome.

SEEK JOY OVER HAPPINESS

When asked for their Why behind attending therapy, most people answer, "I want to be happy." Happiness is an outward expression of emotion. It's fleeting. You can feel it one moment, and it can be gone the next moment. Joy, on the other hand, is internal. It connects you with your purpose for living. And because it's not based on external circumstances, like happiness, it is more sustainable throughout hardships.

Adversity is adversity. What we go through as people is inevitable; you cannot escape the challenges of being a human. But when you look inward to your personal meaning in who you are, you allow joy to shine light on your strengths. You can find this joy by focusing on the things that are going well in your life and practicing gratitude. If you ground your life with gratitude, you make space for joy to guide you through emotions such as anger, sadness, and disappointment. This doesn't invalidate or belittle the bad shit; instead it looks at the good in spite of the bad.

> *I recognized the difference between happiness and joy when I got my first mental health job at a county jail. Having the opportunity to change mental health in the criminal justice system was something I had been dreaming about since watching B.D. Wong on* Law and Order SVU. *I was happy—ecstatic, even. When people asked about my job, I would often say, "I am so happy, I absolutely love what I do." I was happy with the benefits, the work I was doing, and my schedule. Then, shit went left. My supervisor left, and I was asked to step into their role. I was now the supervisor of the mental health department of a county jail at 23 years old with only a bachelor's degree in psychology.*
>
> *My stress levels started to go through the roof as my external environment started to change. I started drinking more and sleeping less, and started having medical problems that led to a colonoscopy at 23. As a supervisor, I had more responsibility,*

which increased my stress. I had to meet with the warden to discuss policies, oversee the suicide watch program, communicate with the onsite psychiatrist, coordinate medications with the nurses, and train the new hires. They even shifted my hours from working Monday through Friday to working weekends as well. On top of all this, I was starting my master's program. I was no longer feeling happiness. Instead, I was angry, stressed, and highly irritable. I was now unhappy.

With hindsight, I recognize that I was focusing on happiness when I should've been focusing on joy. I thought that having a supervisor role would make me happy. I thought being in meetings with people like the warden would make me feel important and happy. But that all depended on my external environment. Because I wasn't experiencing joy, there was nothing to sustain me through the anger, stress, and irritability. Searching for happiness felt like searching for a four-leaf clover in a field of three-leaf clovers.

And then the unthinkable happened: I was let go for asking to step down from the supervisor position. The stress of the role had gotten to me, and my health was declining. At that time, I was planning my wedding, so losing my job felt like the worst thing that could have happened. Or so I thought. After the initial shock wore off, I realized I felt relieved. I wasn't happy about losing my job, but I was grateful that I no longer had the stress related to the job.

Looking back, it was joy that carried me through the loss of my job. When I thought I couldn't afford something for my wedding, I found a way to make it work and was grateful that I could still have a wedding. I had more time to focus on my education and spend time with my fiancé. My internal purpose at the time was to work toward becoming a mental health expert unlike any I had seen before: authentic, bold, gregarious, and eccentric. And guess what? My gastro issues went away.

Choosing to seek joy in your life gives your Why a purpose. It brings your Why into a greater perspective. A part of implementing change outside the therapy room is seeking joy. Manhunt the shit out of joy.

HOW DO YOU SEEK JOY?

Practice gratitude. When something happens, acknowledge the emotions you feel. And after, only after, acknowledging the emotions, ask yourself, "What am I grateful for?" I was devastated when my dog passed away. I let myself sulk in bed with my grief for days. And then I asked myself, "What am I grateful for?" I was grateful that I was no longer living with the uncertainty of when my dog would pass. My dog had been diagnosed with cancer and given six months to live. After I received the news about his diagnosis, I became highly anxious, not knowing when he would pass. I wasn't sure if I would wake up and he would be passed away at the foot of my bed. Or if I would go to work and then return home to him passed away on the couch. I didn't know if I had six months with him or if he could surpass the six months. I was also grateful that he blessed my life with doggy kisses and cuddles for 11 years. Practicing gratitude doesn't mean that you invalidate what you are feeling. And yes, I am Black and let my dog kiss me; don't come for me.

What are you thankful for? Every day might not be a good day, but there is good in every day. You just have to find it. When you start out practicing gratitude, it may not feel comfortable, especially if you are in a place where you aren't happy. But remember: you aren't searching for happiness, you are seeking joy.

Define your Why for existing. To identify if joy is present, consider a role in your life that sometimes brings you happiness. Maybe that role is being a parent. That shit is hard. You may have days when your child comes up to you and hugs you tight with those little hands and squeezes your face as they look into your eyes, and that makes you feel happy. But there are also days when you just wanna use noise-canceling headphones because your 3-year-old is upset you ran out of ketchup for their chicken fries and is now crying hysterically on the floor. So, ask yourself: Why am I a parent?

You must look inward for this answer. *I am a parent because I wanted to raise a child.* Great, now go deeper. Why did you want to have kids? *I wanted to have kids because I wanted to give someone the life I didn't have as a child.* Perfect, keep going. *I didn't feel nurtured when I was a child and I want my child to feel nurtured.* Aha. There it is—you find joy in nurturing your child. Even when they have that tantrum, you still love them and nurture them. Every day, you get up and find joy in nurturing your child. This isn't to say that your child won't upset or annoy you.

Be present in your daily life. Being present means engaging your thoughts and feelings with what is happening in the moment. It means pausing and embracing the moment instead of thinking about the past or future. You are more likely to use the skills and tools that you learned in therapy when present. Looking into the past and future is helpful, but spending too much time there means rarely engaging with what is happening in the here and now.

Let's say you hate your job, but you look forward to lunch with your coworker bestie. If you are present during the lunch, instead of discussing how you hated coming into work (past) and can't wait 'til 5 o'clock to punch out (future), you will focus on interacting in the moment and enjoying your bestie's presence. Maybe you laugh at memes and check in with how you both are doing. The best part is that this can possibly be a moment of gratitude: "I'm grateful for a moment with my bestie during the workday."

Create a music playlist that makes you happy. I understand that seeking joy will take practice and require unlearning, so here's a quick way to experience joy—a playlist of songs that put a smile on your face. Now play this playlist when you are not feeling happy. This will create joy. Although you may not be happy in the moment, you internally experience joy by taking the time to do something that makes you feel happy. You turn inward, away from your external circumstances.

SURROUND YOURSELF WITH DOPE-A$$ PEOPLE

You are the company you keep. Have you ever heard this statement? We don't realize how true it is until we start to take a look at the people in our immediate support system. Surrounding yourself with dope-a$$ people means having people in your corner who will uplift you, see you, offer advice and opinions in an empathetic way, and offer emotional support.

To choose your support system, you first have to identify where your current support system is strong and where changes are needed. Committing to yourself means surrounding yourself with people who embrace you yesterday, today, and tomorrow. Ask yourself, "Are my personal relationships strong enough to adapt to my personal growth?" The purpose of a support system isn't to ONLY have positive relationships; it is to have personal relationships that are healthy for you. A healthy support system will allow for more joy in your life, which can help reduce symptoms of anxiety, post-traumatic stress disorder, and depression, to name a few. It can also help you improve your social and coping skills.

PS, Just because someone is a blood relative does not automatically give them access to your system. People need a wristband. The longevity of a friendship doesn't count either; we are looking at the quality of the relationship. Conduct an interpersonal inventory by taking a look at each personal relationship, labeling its purpose, clarifying how it operates, and identifying how it fits your needs and wants.

DOPE EXERCISE: INTERPERSONAL INVENTORY

Choose a person in your life.

- *How close are you to this person?*
- *How close would this person say they are to you?*
- *How do you feel when you are with this person?*
- *What are the satisfying parts of your relationship with this person?*
- *What are the dissatisfying parts of your relationship with this person?*
- *When you change, will your relationship with this person be sustainable?*

You might need a support system shift if you felt unsettled while responding to those questions or if you didn't like your responses.

Now, identify three to four different areas of your life that you would like support in. (One of these areas should be a hobby.) For me, these are TikTok, parenting, and business. Using the definition of a support system mentioned previously, identify the people who support you in these areas. You need to have at least one different person for each category so that one person is not your only support system.

If you find yourself struggling to identify people in your support system, let's dive into how to build your support system. Once you have identified the three to four areas, ask yourself: "What do I need in each of these areas?" For TikTok, I need someone who appreciates the creativity of creators on the app and understands the challenges of trying to push out content on a daily basis. For parenting, I need someone who is not judgmental and easy to talk to when I am struggling. For my business, I need someone who understands what it is like to own a therapy private practice. Now that you have identified your needs, you'll want to see if there is anyone in your life who can meet those needs. If the answer is no, it's time to put yourself out there and meet new people.

You will do this by putting yourself in the environments where you are likely to meet these people. If I am looking for another friend who is a mom, I may sign up for a parent-child class. If I am looking for support on TikTok, I would look for someone who is also my friend on TikTok and start to interact with them more. To find someone who owns a therapy private practice, I may research private practices in my area and reach out to the owners to start to make a connection. Or I could find events to attend, such as a seminar or convention for private practice owners.

Just as relationships can impact us in positive and healthy ways, they can also impact us in negative and toxic ways. While you go through the therapy process, you might find that you cannot handle certain relationships with other people who are going through their own mental health journey. I want to emphasize that I am not saying you shouldn't be friends with people because they are struggling. What I am saying is that you should recognize when other people's "stuff" starts to affect you. For example, if you struggle with thoughts of self-harm and have a friend who frequently talks about their own thoughts of self-harm with you, your friend could trigger you. This may not be healthy for you.

How do you remove yourself if you find that one of your personal relationships isn't healthy for you? First, decide if you want to have a conversation with the other person about why the relationship isn't healthy for you. If you decide no conversation is needed, it may be helpful to briefly let them know that you are moving in a different direction personally. If you decide yes, choose a neutral space (not your space or their space) to have the conversation. Use "I" statements to effectively communicate how you arrived at the decision, why you are making the decision, what that means for the relationship, and how the relationship will look moving forward. Please, don't try to sugarcoat. Being clear and not sugarcoating can look like this: "I feel that where I am in my life, I have to make decisions that are healthy for me. Right now, a healthy decision is choosing to take space from our relationship. I chose this decision because I am easily triggered when there is talk about self-harm and I struggle to come back from that place. At this time, I think it is best if we take a step back. This means I will not be having contact for right now. I don't know if it'll always be that way, but this is what is best for me right now." Do you know what you just did? You set a boundary. That's definitely worth a therapy twerk.

SET BOUNDARIES

Setting boundaries is for everyone. Boundaries separate you from others; they are mental, physical, and emotional limits that you set around yourself. Boundaries protect you from being taken advantage of and allow you to have healthy relationships with yourself and others.

In therapy, you will learn more about what your needs and wants are, how others meet your needs, and how people don't meet your needs or violate your needs. When you learn more about how other people impact and affect you, you can now use your skills and tools to teach people how to treat you and interact with you.

WHY ARE BOUNDARIES IMPORTANT?

If you don't set boundaries, you may find yourself being injured physically, mentally, and emotionally. It can be a struggle to implement boundaries because you may not know how or where to place them. In his book *Not Nice,* Dr. Aziz Gazipura states that a lack of boundaries comes from niceness. What he is getting at is that a lack of boundaries comes from the desire to be nice to others. It is the inaccurate formula: "If I please others, give them everything they want, keep a low profile, and don't ruffle feathers or create any discomfort, then others will like me, love me, and shower me with approval and everything else I want." Boundaries are about being nice to yourself. Let's say you have a coworker who keeps coming to your desk for small talk. This makes you feel frustrated and annoyed because it throws you off from work. Your emotions are telling you that a boundary is needed. Boundaries are for you regardless of how other people respond to them. The only people who don't like boundaries are those who benefit from you not having any. Also, setting boundaries doesn't mean you have beef with someone.

TYPES OF BOUNDARIES

There are several types of boundaries: physical, emotional, mental, time, and nonnegotiables. Physical boundaries have to do with your body. They can encompass your preferred comfort levels regarding physical contact, such as interacting with people, sleep, sex, and what you eat. You may notice a boundary is needed when you feel uncomfortable or uneasy.

You may not notice that an emotional or mental boundary is needed until after the boundary is crossed. These types of boundaries tell people how to talk to you or treat you. For example, you could set an emotional and mental boundary by saying no to emotional dumping and leaving the conversation, or by telling people how you feel about the way they talk to you and letting them know that if they don't change the way they talk to you, you will walk away. Telling the other person about your boundary is only the first half of setting the boundary. It must be followed by action that lets the person know "this is what happens when my boundary is not respected." You are not responsible for taking care of others' feelings related to your setting of boundaries. That friend who hinders your sleep by calling in the middle of the night to dump on you . . . boundary! That in-law who wants to discuss politics at Christmas . . . boundary! That boss who asks about your hair . . . boundary!

Time and knowledge boundaries are my favorite boundaries because everybody and they momma be trying to get on your calendar these days. Talkin' 'bout, "I only need 15 minutes," knowing damn well it could have been an email (*side eye*). Or we all love a "Can I pick your brain?" Sometimes a good *hell naw* is needed. Time is precious and it doesn't slow down for anyone. Your knowledge was earned through your life experiences, and if you went to school, through education. Guard your time and knowledge like they're newborn babies. You may not recognize that you need to define time and knowledge boundaries until they have been crossed. Pay attention to how you respond both emotionally and physically. Sometimes your body may tell you that a boundary is needed before your mind can process it.

And then we have nonnegotiable boundaries. These are related to situations that you are not okay with being flexible around, the ones where the answer is always no. Usually nonnegotiable boundaries are related to feeling safe. Look at these as deal breakers. They can cover issues like infidelity, abuse, drugs, or something that would threaten your life. Nonnegotiable boundaries can also encompass the other boundaries mentioned earlier.

HOW DO YOU SET BOUNDARIES?

Recognize when you need a boundary. Your mind usually warns you when you need boundaries through emotional charges that feel hard to control. You may notice this if you feel that something has ruined your day, or you want to go off on someone.

You may also recognize that you need boundaries in other ways: if you notice yourself engaging with negative behaviors; if you feel emotionally charged toward a person, place, or situation; if something triggers you; or if you experience a sudden change in attitude. Pausing and asking yourself, "How is this place (or person) making me feel?" will usually give you insight into whether a boundary is needed or not.

Define the boundary. Once you determine that setting a boundary is necessary, you need to define it. Define what it looks like, why you are implementing it, and how it relates to your Why. After defining it, ask yourself: "What do I hope to accomplish by putting this boundary in place?" Labeling what you hope to accomplish will bring into view whether or not the boundary is realistic. Then, you want to identify how it protects you. You will eventually put your boundary into action, so being able to identify how it protects you serves as motivation to see it through.

Implement the boundary. Use "I" statements when communicating your boundary to others. When you use "you" statements, you may quickly find yourself taking care of other people's feelings, and that's not what we are here for. For example, instead of saying, "You hurt my feelings when you talk to me like that," use an "I" statement: "I don't like when you talk to me that way. I feel hurt, and therefore I won't allow it." And then whip around and walk away like a badass. When you set a boundary and use "I" statements, you take responsibility for yourself.

For those of you who feel apprehensive about setting boundaries, strike when the iron is cold. This means letting someone know about your boundary after the moment has happened and you feel less emotionally charged. Being in a calmer state of mind allows you to effectively communicate your boundaries. Not saying anything is also a boundary. Blocking can send a message, if you feel me. Start by setting small boundaries that allow you to work up to the larger ones.

Process and reflect. Now you can return to therapy and process how it went. You can process what it was like implementing the boundary, the results of the boundary, and whether it will be a flexible boundary or a nonnegotiable one. If the boundary didn't work, you may receive validation and support from your therapist that furthers your motivation to continue to work on boundaries. Or maybe the boundary worked and you find yourself feeling more comfortable. You learned what your needs and wants were and how to fulfill them. But you wouldn't have found yourself at this place if you hadn't put in the effort outside of the session.

YOU MAY LACK BOUNDARIES IF . . .

- You feel bad when you say no.
- You don't speak up when you are treated in a way that you perceive as wrong.
- You feel overwhelmed by other people.
- You try to please other people.
- You neglect yourself by trying to be nice to other people.
- You touch people or allow yourself to be touched without permission.
- You're not honest with other people about how you feel.
- You compromise your own values and morals for others.
- You allow others to take from you.

Muranda notices that her 6-year-old, Aria, gets closed off every time she hugs her grandpa. Muranda hadn't been taught about physical boundaries growing up. In her family, when an elder asks for a hug, you give them one. Coz when you don't, the adult often hugs you anyway and says, "Oh girl, come give yo grandma a hug, you know me." Lately, Muranda has been discussing boundaries in her therapy sessions. She remembers that growing up, she would also feel uncomfortable about giving hugs to people she didn't want to hug. Because of her upbringing, whenever she questioned hugging, she was told, "Don't be disrespectful." Now, Muranda struggles to use her voice, even when it comes to standing up for her child.

Muranda practices how to say no and set boundaries in therapy through role-play with her therapist. She decides to set a boundary by asking Aria's grandpa to ask Aria for permission before going in for a hug. The next time grandpa comes over, he goes right in to give Aria a hug. But Muranda, for the first time, stops him and says "No." She then reminds him of what they talked about around the hug boundary. He can choose to ask or not go for a hug at all. Muranda feels uncomfortable at first, but later on, she feels empowered, especially after seeing how her daughter opens up more around grandpa. She realizes her inability to set boundaries and say no was due to what was modeled for her growing up.

IDENTIFY AND RESPOND TO YOUR EMOTIONS

Emotions can run the show if you let them; it'll be a whole-a$$ monologue. Therapy sessions are spent discussing, labeling, and identifying your emotions. With this, you gain clarity and insight into why you feel the way you do. You get to decide what to do with this newfound insight once you leave your therapist's office.

Whenever you are in a situation that evokes emotions, label how you feel so that you can understand where you are emotionally. Once you identify an emotion, observe it both mentally and physically. How are you physically feeling in the moment? Heart racing? Jaw clenched? This process slows you down to be present in the moment and lets you choose a response. Focusing on the emotion and your thoughts behind it will help you identify the action you want to take. Next, accept your emotions. There is no such thing as a negative emotion. Your feelings are always valid; welcome them.

Now, after pausing to identify, clarify, and acknowledge your emotions, you can choose how you want to respond. This pause is the crucial difference between reacting and responding. Reacting is impulsive and can come from a place of hurt and defensiveness. When we come from this place, we may feel better in the moment. However, upon reflecting, we often find that our impulsive reactions didn't resolve anything internally and potentially externally. When you respond, you intentionally choose how you want to behave in the situation and ultimately ensure a much better outcome.

PRACTICE SELF-LOVE

Self-care has been turned into a social media trend. It shows up on our feeds as images of people taking lavish vacations, reading a book with the sun glistening off their hair, or smiling candidly while walking their dog. Because of social media, the trend has left people feeling like they aren't doing self-care right. That's why I say self-love instead of self-care. The purpose of self-care is to take care of yourself in a way that shows you either love or are working on loving yourself. However, the purpose of self-love is to do things to keep yourself healthy physically, mentally, and emotionally. Through self-love, you build and maintain a healthy relationship with yourself.

But why is it important to practice self-love? Therapy can be draining as a mofo and can sometimes leave you feeling exhausted by the end of your sessions. Because you are exerting energy in therapy, your body requires you to replenish it when you're not in therapy. Taking care of yourself through self-love work will help sustain the therapy journey.

What does self-love look like? A great place to start is by identifying your physical, mental, and emotional needs. Self-love works best when all three categories are hit. Are you feeling drained at work? Are you feeling lonely in your relationships? Once you identify your needs, it's time to figure out how you can meet them on your own. This is a skill that may take time, but it's worth it.

Maybe you go for a walk while listening to inspiring podcasts. Or maybe you play with your dog while listening to an audiobook. Or maybe you meditate while doing breath work. Breathing counts as physical movement in my book. (Just don't tell my personal trainer.)

DOPE EXAMPLES OF SELF-LOVE

EMOTIONAL	PHYSICAL	MENTAL
Journaling	Walking	Meditating
Calling your support system	Taking a dance class	Breathing exercises
Reading	Stretching	Practicing mindfulness
Going to therapy	Using progressive muscle relaxation	Practicing gratitude
Asking for help	Sex	
Setting boundaries	Yoga	
Limiting exposure to news media	Sleeping	

DOPE EXPERT: DR. KRISTEN CASEY
(@drkristencasey)

I want to especially place emphasis on sleep. A lack of sleep can severely impact us both in life and in therapy. Let's talk to Kristen Casey, a clinical psychologist specializing in sleep. I got a feeling she's going to lay our edges with knowledge.

> Kristen, we need your help! Can you help us understand how not managing sleep can affect our mental health? What happens when someone stays up late but still has to get up early?

Damn, where do I begin? I think of the concept of sleep deprivation (e.g., being awake for several days), and then those of us who don't prioritize our relationship with sleep (way more common). If we focus on the latter, we notice increased irritability, cognitive fog, physical fatigue, and low energy. On a deeper level, some of us might feel inadequate, insecure, or shameful about the fact that we can't just "get with it" after lack of sleep. Ever hate yourself the next morning because you knew better? But scrolling on TikTok was more important at the time?

We also know that if we already have excessive stress, depression, anxiety, burnout, or PTSD, this might make our symptoms more pronounced. We aren't exactly ourselves when we're exhausted, and it's important to note that sleep hygiene is within our control. Sometimes we can't control our life circumstances and the reasons why we are depressed, but we can certainly get a handle on helpful sleep hygiene.

I hear you on sleep hygiene, but how can we put boundaries around our sleep routines?

The easiest thing to do, even though you'll hate me for it, is this: get up at the exact same time every day. *Consistency.* Yeah, even on the weekends. Our body starts operating like a machine when we're consistent.

When we wake up at the same time each day, our body's biological process becomes a routine. Yup, bowel movements, melatonin secretion, and those internal cues of sleepiness that we all desire (eyes getting heavy, nodding off at night). We can't expect ourselves to fall asleep at the same time every night if we aren't waking up at the same time each morning.

Sleep is important—got it. Create boundaries around your routine—got it. But where do we start?

Recognizing that you're exhausted and have trouble falling asleep or staying asleep is the first step. Keep in mind, there are over 70 sleep disorders, and these suggestions focus mainly on insomnia.

Chronic insomnia is when you experience difficulty falling or staying asleep, wake up before your intended alarm, experience dissatisfaction with the quality of your sleep, or worry about your sleep health at least three times a week for three months. (If you have these experiences for less than three months, it is acute insomnia.) The following are resources for improved sleep hygiene.

Sleep Information: The National Sleep Foundation (sleepfoundation. org) is a great place to start if you want more reliable, credible information about managing sleep. If you notice that you're having difficulties attending events or getting things done because of sleepiness, it might be helpful to see a professional.

Insomnia Treatment: There are providers around that specialize in this modality. You might also need to speak with your primary care physician about medications if this is a newer issue.

Insomnia Coaching: There are a few apps that focus on insomnia coaching, such as Dawn Health (www.dawn.health). This is not the same as therapy, but it's an accessible option for people who want to work on their insomnia goals. Their app is backed by research, and they work with amazing sleep professionals, which is a total plus. This is one of my favorite apps when someone tells me they can't afford therapy but want reliable help.

SAY NO WHEN YOU NEED TO

Did you know that saying no is also a way to practice self-love? It can hit the mental and emotional category, and if you roll your neck with it, maybe even the physical category. But all jokes aside, saying no is something that many people don't think of. It ticks the boundary box and the self-love box. Saying no also builds your confidence. If you practice saying no outside of the session, you can now come into the session to process how it went. This will allow for validation and feedback. If you are trying to figure out what areas of your life to practice saying no in, start by asking yourself: "Where do I feel uncomfortable in my life?"

Outside the session is where most of the action work will take place. The processing that you do in the sessions helps you identify where you need boundaries, what's not bringing you joy, and what it looks like to have supportive people in your life. If you read this chapter and are currently in therapy, it may be helpful to have a conversation with your therapist to ask where you can start to implement the tools and skills outside the session.

DOPE TAKEAWAYS

» Evaluate the people in your life.

» Seek joy over happiness.

» Set boundaries—they are there to protect you.

» Identify your emotions to choose a responsive behavior.

» Practice self-love by taking care of yourself physically, mentally, and emotionally.

» Say no when you are uncomfortable.

CHAPTER EIGHT

TRAUMA

"my mind keeps running off to dark corners and coming back with reasons for why i am not enough"

—RUPI KAUR, *HOME BODY*

only took one trauma course in grad school. Twenty-four-year-old Shani would tell you it was because I didn't recognize the crucial need to understand trauma and because the one class I took required the longest paper I had ever written in my academic career. Shani today has the words to effectively describe why I only took the one class: that long-ass paper and the fact that academic literature at the time did not represent trauma for Black people.

In grad school, I was only taught about extreme cases of trauma that surrounded post-traumatic stress disorder (PTSD) diagnoses and dissociative identity disorder. I saw trauma as rape and war—that's it. I wasn't taught to understand that you can experience trauma without having a diagnosis. The people represented in the course literature were usually white people and veterans. There wasn't much attention given to Black people, the LGBTQ+ community, immigrants—basically the entire minority population. I would spend a great deal of my academic career learning and believing that trauma only occurred externally and in extreme states.

TRAUMA-INFORMED VS. TRAUMA-TRAINED

Healing from trauma begins with the right therapist, one who specializes in trauma and has been trained to work with clients who suffer from trauma. When I say trained, I don't mean therapists who went to a weekend EMDR (eye movement desensitization and reprocessing) training or have a trauma certificate from their academic institution. I am referring to therapists who have had extensive and explicit training, supervision, and experience working directly with trauma.

I am not a trauma-trained therapist. I am a trauma-informed therapist. A trauma-informed therapist understands how trauma can present and may know a few interventions. However, if you are primarily attending therapy to work on your trauma, you need a trauma-trained therapist. A lot of people can find themselves in therapy for an extended period of time because they're not receiving the right kind of care. You may not be aware as a client coming into the therapy room, but it is the therapist's responsibility to communicate when they are out of the scope of practice. An ethical therapist will be upfront and honest about what they understand and what they are trained in. You can still continue to see your current therapist; however, you need a trauma-trained therapist to safely get to the root of your trauma, understand your trauma, and work through your trauma with evidence-based interventions and treatment services.

YOUR BODY REMEMBERS

Outside of being absent during my childhood, my father has never done anything to intentionally harm me. We had spent a great deal of my adulthood building our relationship and I could spend hours talking to my father about anything from sex and my business, to my marriage and friends. I would say that we now have a GREAT relationship.

In 2020, my father and I decided to drive to Las Vegas for his birthday. It was our first vacation together. I didn't get much sleep the previous night as I usually feel nervous the night before I travel. I figured I would sleep on the ride up. Car rides have always been soothing for me, so you can imagine my surprise when I couldn't sleep. We arrived at the hotel, and I dropped off my father at the door to check in. My stomach dropped as soon as he got out of the car. I remember thinking, "Please get a hotel room with two beds, please please please."

We get to the room and open the door, and I see one king-size bed. Immediately, I felt uncomfortable, and my body became tense. My heart started to race. My dad decided that he was going to head to the cigar bar. I was too exhausted to go and said I would hang back and try to rest before meeting him for dinner. When I climbed into the bed, I put a pillow down the middle. I remember thinking: "Why are you doing this? This is your father. Why are you uncomfortable sharing a bed with your father? This is silly!" I negatively told myself. "Your father has never and would never harm you."

I spent the rest of the evening tossing and turning. Everything in me wanted to run and get my own room. My body's stress responses were kicking in. It felt like my body was on high alert but exhausted at the same time. On day two, after failed attempts to use over-the-counter sleeping aids, I found myself at a dispensary asking for an indica strain.

I don't smoke marijuana because my ass can't figure out the inhale, hold, exhale part to get high, and because of the paranoid side effects I experience, but I was desperate. I had gotten maybe two to three hours of sleep over a 48-hour period. I remember sitting in the hotel room, cracking the window, and smoking, praying that I was smoking it correctly so I could get some ZZZs. Inhale, hold, count to five, exhale. F*ck, I didn't cough . . . I just know I did it wrong. Frustration set in and my body was breaking down. I was afraid of what would happen if I didn't get some sleep soon. I was so afraid of the side effects of no sleep that I found myself on a nurse line, crying that I hadn't slept, tried to smoke weed, and was in Las Vegas. I prayed that they wouldn't think I was just another person who did Vegas wrong.

At that point, I was prescribed hydroxyzine and was finally able to get three to four hours of sleep. The final day in Vegas, I woke up feeling a little more rested. But mentally, nothing had changed. It was like my body had slept but my brain had stayed awake. It was like I knew I was sleeping. I would experience racing thoughts and disturbing images all while I was "sleeping."

After I arrived home, it took my body two to three days and several 12-hour stints of sleeping to come back to homeostasis and feel like myself again. Looking back, I now know that my body was experiencing a trauma response. The remembered trauma in my body had been triggered, and it increased my stress hormone levels while I was in Vegas.

The stress response is flight, fight, and freeze. Remember me saying that I didn't understand why I wasn't sleeping because my father had never done anything to harm me? The thing is, my brain didn't know that. When the stress response is activated, the brain cannot tell the difference between a real or perceived threat. When the brain perceives a threat, the amygdala lights up. As psychiatrist and author Bessel van der Kolk says, "The amygdala is the smoke alarm of the brain." My amygdala was sounding the alarm *all* mofo weekend.

I would later learn that the incident in Vegas was a perceived threat because sharing a bed with a man other than my husband was a reminder of my trauma. And here's why: most of my trauma is sexual and related to men. Why didn't I speak up? Because I didn't want to hurt my father's feelings. I wanted to be nice to him. I didn't want to make him feel uncomfortable, so I didn't set boundaries and remained uncomfortable. This is what I didn't learn about in grad school, that your traumatic response can be triggered by things that resemble your trauma. Thus, sharing a bed with my father was a perceived threat.

When I went full-time at my private practice, my clients mainly consisted of Black women between the ages of 23 and 30. I started to recognize that many of them lacked memories of their childhood. I found that my clients all had a lot in common: low self-esteem, overcompensation in some area of their life, and an impact of their childhood on their finances. As I started to work more with my clients, I realized that many of them had experienced trauma but not in the ways that I had read about in the literature. Most of their trauma was related to race, discrimination, poverty, community violence, and refugee status. It was then that I found myself wanting to study trauma and understand it for me and my people.

~~~~~~

DOPE EXPERT: DR. DESTA (@my_destanation)

Because it is important that the clinicians in the field of mental health represent people of color, I invited Dr. Desta (postdoctoral fellow) to drop some knowledge on trauma for us. Dr. Desta holds a PhD in clinical psychology and provides empowering information about trauma for Black people, Indigenous people, and people of color through her TikTok content. Because trauma evolves and is constantly changing, I asked her to share some signs of unresolved trauma. According to Dr. Desta, these are some indications that you may be dealing with unresolved trauma:

- *Dissociation or detachment from the world around you*

- *Flashbacks, nightmares, or intrusive memories or thoughts*

- *Anxiety, depression, and irritability or anger*

- *Shame or self-blame, such as thoughts of being broken, damaged, or worthless*

- *Avoidance of unpleasant emotions or certain situations*

- *Increase in substance use as an attempt to escape, numb, or mask your emotions*

- *Hypervigilance or feeling on guard*

- *Chronic pain, muscle tension, high blood pressure, or gastrointestinal (GI) distress*

- *Difficulty falling asleep or staying asleep, or waking up earlier than intended*

- *Body memories and somatic re-experiencing (somatic re-experiencing is when a person physically re-experiences trauma, which may come as physical pain, discomfort, or sensations)*

- *Alterations to thoughts related to safety, intimacy, trust, self-esteem, and power or control*

- *Forgetfulness or difficulty concentrating*
- *Difficulty tolerating conflict, confrontation, or criticism*
- *All-or-nothing thinking*

~~~~~~

BIG TRAUMA AND LITTLE TRAUMA

In the mental health world, trauma can be referred to as big T (big trauma) and little T (little trauma). The big T is universally recognizable trauma, usually something that is life-threatening, such as rape or war. Little T is often harder to recognize because it can be traumatic for one person but not another and may not be life-threatening. I did an interview with CBS Minnesota during the time of the George Floyd murder, and I spoke explicitly about racial trauma and how trauma has to be rethought. A PTSD diagnosis isn't culturally sensitive. For one, the exclusion criteria specifies that trauma cannot be experienced while watching TV. But my people, Black people, consistently hear and witness the ongoing murders of our people by white cops through social media, TV broadcasts, and word of mouth.

In 2020, we experienced a worldwide pandemic, and a majority of the world was placed on lockdown. Some were single at the time, living alone and isolated. Many were living through uncertain times and were absorbing critical information through media sources. The only way to receive updates about the pandemic was through media news stations, social media, and newspapers. Hearing about people contracting a contagious disease and dying can be *traumatic*.

"Stress becomes traumatic when danger, risk, fear or anxiety are present," states Patrick Carnes, PhD, founder of the International Institute for Trauma and Addiction Professionals. Between 2020 and now, did you watch a TV broadcast about COVID-19 and feel your heart rate increase, your shoulders tense, or your palms become sweaty? Did you find yourself feeling irritated, angry, or frustrated? I found myself feeling anxious to be in public, but at the same time, my experience monitoring the segregation unit at the jail had made me aware of the harm that extended isolation can cause. Many people shared my experiences. My clients were trying to balance being informed about the pandemic while also trying to monitor their exposure to information. The coverage around COVID-19 was stressful, especially when navigating what was true or false. How many days to isolate? Do you wipe down food when you bring it home from the grocery store? Is hand sanitizer really effective? Navigating this uncertain period was fearful for many people. There was an uptick in anxiety over the stress of the pandemic. We have stress and fear and anxiety; therefore, we can have trauma.

Little trauma may be hard to recognize because not everyone experiences it in the same way. For example, consider the 2020 presidential election. For some people, the 2020 election was merely another voting season. For others, our lives depended on it. For me, the election was about whether or not I could feel safe in America. My little T trauma with the election started when I saw Trump supporters, most of them white. Their signs indicated that they didn't care about my life. In response to seeing them, I yelled "BLACK LIVES MATTER." As votes were being counted, I remember thinking, *Is my family going to be safe in America for the next four years?* My beautiful, shea butter-smelling melanin skin no longer felt safe.

Shortly after Biden was officially elected, my stress increased. Trump supporters were furious, and I felt especially unsafe around them in Arizona. This was apparent to me as I rode my bike around 8 p.m. one night. I often exercise when I am stressed; it's my coping skill. When I first exited my apartment, I was in the bike lane. But then my body kicked into flight mode. Everything was telling me to get on the sidewalk. My electric bike can clock 29 mph, and I knew it wasn't safe for pedestrians if I was on the sidewalk, so I got back to the bike lane. Immediately, my intrusive thoughts started, *WHAT IF A TRUMP SUPPORTER SEES YOU RIDING AT NIGHT AND THEY HIT*

*YOU AND GET AWAY WITH IT BECAUSE IT'S DARK? YOU WILL NEVER
SEE YOUR CHILDREN AGAIN, GET ON THE FUCKING SIDEWALK!*
I spent a great deal of that bike ride going from sidewalk to bike
lane, bike lane to sidewalk. My body was reacting to my thoughts,
and my brain had perceived that my bike ride was a threat. I knew
the elections had been a traumatic experience for me when my
concern was about a Trump supporter seeing me and purposefully
hurting me because I'm Black.

Little traumas are distressing to the person experiencing them.
Other examples of little traumas could be the death of pet, a
Black person being told to change their hair at work, bullying, or
harassment. These events affect an individual person, which is why
they fall under little traumas.

RISK FACTORS VS. PROTECTIVE FACTORS

Two people can experience the exact same trauma event and walk
away from it with completely different reactions. Each individual
responds based on their protective factors and their risk factors.
When we talk about risk factors, we're talking about things that
decrease your ability to cope with traumatic events. Risk factors
may be an adverse childhood experience, current life stressors,
income, and quite frankly, being part of the BIPOC community.

> *Joshua grew up in Harvey, Illinois, with his grandmother,
> Deloris. Drive-by shootings and poverty weren't new to him.
> During Joshua's youth, his grandmother struggled to take care
> of him and his siblings after his mom passed away. He got into a
> lot of trouble because he would steal things and resell them to
> put food on the table. He was afraid that if he didn't help his
> grandmother, the state would put him and his siblings back in
> foster care. In addition, he would have outbursts at school. His
> falling asleep in class was perceived as defiant. Due to his
> school's lack of cultural humility, Joshua was labeled a child with*

behavioral problems. The school's social worker diagnosed him with oppositional defiant disorder (ODD).

When Joshua starts therapy as an adult, he learns that he has PTSD from his childhood. He is surprised; he had no idea that he had experienced trauma as a child. He had seen his life as the norm for Black boys in his neighborhood, just a way of surviving. His therapist points out that his socioeconomic status and lack of support were risk factors. For the first time, Joshua has the language to describe what was going on.

This is why cultural humility is important. If Joshua's school had a social worker who practiced cultural humility, they would have looked into his home life to understand why he was falling asleep, stealing, and having outbursts.

DOPE EXPERT: DR. DESTA (@my_destanation)

I asked our dope expert Dr. Desta what cultural humility can look like from a therapeutic approach, and y'all, she gave me the lesson I needed in grad school.

Dr. Desta, can you give us the tea on what cultural humility can look like from a therapeutic approach when doing trauma work?

Anti-oppressive frameworks are needed when using trauma-specific treatments because trauma responses are impacted by culture. By utilizing an anti-oppressive framework, therapists can also broaden their definition of trauma when assessing their patients to include more than the DSM's definition of a criterion A trauma. Therapists need to also review their measures and alter their intervention strategies to ensure that they are culturally sensitive.

An anti-oppressive framework requires therapists to do a lot of self-reflection on possible biases, assumptions, and blind spots and how they may impact their therapeutic relationships with marginalized patients; therapists need to confront their own beliefs. The patient is not responsible for educating the therapist. And at the end of the day, impact matters more than intent. The therapist needs to be receptive to feedback, validate the client's experience, and take responsibility for the impact of the therapist's actions.

Okay, I hear you loud and clear, but what would you say to someone who is apprehensive to opening the door to their trauma?

It's common and expected for you to be nervous about starting therapy or disclosing your trauma for the first time. The unknown is anxiety provoking; you are not alone in that! Remember, therapy is meant to add someone to your corner to support you throughout the process. Talking with your therapist can help you feel seen, heard, and valued, and you deserve to experience that. As a therapist, I feel honored when my patients disclose their trauma to me because I get to hear their story; that's a privilege. As a client, sharing my story with my therapist helped me to reclaim the parts of myself that trauma took from me and find a path to healing. And remember, at the end of the day, you are in control. As a therapist, we will always prioritize your choice, safety, and trust in the therapeutic relationship. Both sides have a shared goal of collaboration and empowerment.

Okay, so we open the door; how can we take care of ourselves while doing trauma work?

Some of these strategies may help:

- *Grounding techniques to help reassure yourself that you are in the present*

- *Self-soothe kit that has tools to provide yourself comfort*
- *Scheduled decompression time after sessions for radical self-care for body, mind, and spirit*
- *Journaling in between sessions to discover connections between past and present*
- *Mindfulness to help you nonjudgmentally focus on the present moment and on your experience*

Think about the things in your life that have affected the way that you respond to stressors. For instance, when the pandemic hit, some companies let people go. Others took away benefits. They removed 401(k) plans, cut insurance benefits, reduced paid time off, and decreased pay. An individual's response to those stressors would depend on what was going on in their life at the time. Let's say you had been drowning in debt and were just barely making ends meet. The inability to make ends meet can be considered a risk factor that reduced your ability to cope when your job decreased pay during the pandemic.

We can't forget about protective factors. Protective factors diminish the onset of PTSD by increasing your ability to cope with traumatic events. If you experienced a pay decrease during the pandemic, your protective factors might have been unemployment benefits or support from your family.

When my dog died in 2020, I swear I thought the universe was trippin'. I kept pleading with 2020 to please not take my dog, but it did. The audacity of the Universe. I had never put down a dog before, and watching my dog go limp in my arms ranked high for traumatic experiences, another little T for the books. My response to this event would have been very different if I hadn't had some protective factors in place.

One of my protective factors was a banging support system. Although my husband was going through the loss at the same time, he was so supportive of me. He supported me as I lay in bed all day, and he brought me food. (In case I didn't tell you, my zodiac sign is Taurus, so food is priority.) In addition, I received amazing DMs from my community on TikTok and Instagram; everyone was so supportive and validating of what I was going through. Another protective factor at that time was my income. I was able to take time off without worrying about how I was going to make ends meet. In addition, I could afford to go to therapy to process my grieving. My income afforded me the opportunity to really take the time to focus on grieving.

YOUR BRAIN ON TRAUMA

Y'all, we're about to get a little sciencey up in here. It's important that you understand how your brain works, a.k.a. the neuroscience of trauma, as knowing what is happening internally allows for better understanding and less self-blame. It also allows room for you to give yourself grace, because I know that when you're going through this healing process, you can sometimes think, "Why am I this way?"

There are three parts to the brain: reptilian (brain stem), mammalian (limbic, midbrain), and the human brain (neocortex). The reptilian brain is responsible for your survival instincts and automatic body responses. The mammalian brain is responsible for emotions and sensory relays. Then there is the most highly evolved part of our brains, the neocortex. This part of the brain controls cognitive processing, decision-making, learning, memory, and inhibitory functions. When we experience a traumatic event, the reptilian brain takes over. At this point, your body starts to increase production of stress hormones; you are now prepared for fight, flight, or freeze. This is why someone who is diagnosed with PTSD is constantly reactive when triggered; their reptilian brain is in the driver's seat.

There are several areas of the brain that can be affected when trauma hits. The first area is the amygdala. You know that loud-a$$ alarm in your house that goes off annoyingly when it is out of battery? Yeah, consider that your amygdala. Remember that the amygdala is the smoke alarm of the brain. When a traumatic event happens and presents danger toward you in a physical, mental, or emotional way, your amygdala is like "Yo, wake up, wake up, trauma, danger!" It lets you know that you need to respond.

The amygdala can become overactive after a traumatic event. It activates your stress response and rushes adrenaline throughout your body. If the amygdala is overactive, you will experience a heightened fear response, which can increase anxiety and disable rational responses. The memory of that event is then imprinted on the amygdala, hence the body holding trauma. The amygdala will remember this experience, including the intensity of the emotions you felt. For example, suppose you were bitten by a dog and found it to be traumatic, and you then see a picture of a dog in a book. Your amygdala may go off ("Yo . . . dog . . . close the book!") because your brain cannot distinguish between a real or a perceived threat, like when I was with my father in Vegas. Your brain may not know that you're seeing a picture of a dog, and it's not a real dog with the potential to harm you. A trauma-trained therapist will work with you to decrease the activation of your amygdala.

You know the movie *Inside Out*? Remember the scene where they had all the memory balls? If you struggle to remember your childhood, there's a possibility that your hippocampus took some time off. The job of the hippocampus is to store our memories. When trauma happens, the hippocampus may involuntarily push a stored memory relating to that trauma into your consciousness, causing you to experience it in the present. If you find yourself having flashbacks about something that happened to you in the past, yell at your hippocampus. Tell that bish she had one job and that was to keep your past memories in the past.

The prefrontal cortex (PFC) is the HBIC (head bitch in charge) when it comes to thinking, and she's a badass when regulated. She helps you if you need to concentrate or make a decision. When you anticipate the events in your environment, that is the PFC at work. Controlling your impulses and managing your emotions are also parts of her job. For those who have experienced trauma, the PFC may be underactive, leading to impulsive decisions, negative thinking patterns, an inability to connect with others, and difficulty concentrating.

TYPES OF TRAUMAS

We know that trauma can be seen as big T and little T, and that it can affect our brain, but there are also different types of traumas.

Collective trauma is when a group of people experience trauma together. The murders of George Floyd, Breonna Taylor, Trayvon Martin, and Daunte Wright are just scratching the surface of the collective trauma that Black people have experienced. Another example of collective trauma is 9/11. In the show *Squid Game*, the players of the game can also be considered a collective trauma.

I'm working on how I talk to my children about Black Lives Matter because if I don't, my narrative can turn into *intergenerational trauma.* This type of trauma is handed down from one generation to another through behaviors or stories. My narrative incorporates feeling unsafe in primarily white spaces, such as certain businesses, which I often heard my relatives talk about. I remember immediately feeling unsafe when one of my favorite coffee shops announced on Instagram that they backed the blue. When my daughter asked why we could no longer get her favorite galaxy lemonade from that coffee shop, I consciously considered how to explain to her why I felt unsafe without passing the trauma down to her.

When George Floyd was murdered, I remember numbing myself. I had just moved away from Minneapolis ten days prior. I couldn't allow myself to fall apart. How the hell was I supposed to be there for my clients throughout the coming weeks if I fell apart? I absorbed the fears and anxieties of my Black clients living in Minneapolis. When they talked about their traumatic protesting experiences, I often found myself short of breath, tense, and trying to practice breathing exercises.

You know the craziest part about this? The DSM-5 actually excludes from its PTSD criteria any trauma experienced from hearing about a traumatic event. It states that the diagnosis "does not apply to exposure through electric media, television, movies, or pictures, unless the exposure is work related." In doing so, it excludes generational trauma. I think about the children of Holocaust survivors, about little Black boys, about immigrants, about all of the narratives that have impacted lives as they are passed down through generations. How the f*ck do you exclude so many populations?

Most of us are aware of the slave history in America. I say "most of us" because not everyone knows the true story. Our school system teaches it in a manner that makes it easily digestible, encouraging people to forget the traumatic impact it had on the Black community. That, my readers, is an example of *historical trauma.*

Some white people struggle to understand why Black people don't trust white people, and my simple answer to that is historical trauma. "I didn't know," is what I sometimes hear from white people. But then I ask myself: Were they not sitting in the same classroom as Black children when slavery was taught? And then I think: "Aha, their families are not discussing the truth of events within their homes." Black people get the version of how we were enslaved, beaten, and raped, and although slavery was abolished, there is still racism. Who did the beating? White people! Who enslaved us? White people! Since that's the case, are white great-grandparents and grandparents not discussing this history in their homes? Coz in Black homes we get the traumatic version, because being naive can get us killed.

There is also a type of trauma called *complex trauma.* Complex trauma is repeated and prolonged exposure to the traumatic event. Examples of complex trauma could include the experience of being kidnapped or a young child experiencing repeated molestation.

I know we just discussed some heavy stuff, and I want you to check in with yourself. What are you feeling? This work can easily trigger you. Because of that, if you need a moment before moving on, please take a pause. When you are ready, let's talk about next steps.

WHAT NOW?

You know the definition of trauma, how trauma can be experienced, how it affects your brain, and that a trauma-trained therapist is needed. But how do you start to work on your trauma? It's normal if you are feeling apprehensive. Trauma work needs to be addressed in a safe environment. As Dr. Desta says, "As a therapist, I feel honored when my patients disclose their trauma to me because I get to hear their story; that's a privilege. As a client, sharing my story with my therapist helped me to reclaim the parts of myself that trauma took from me and find a path to healing."

When you start working on your trauma, it is essential that you take care of yourself. For trauma, Dr. Desta emphasizes grounding techniques. The trauma you process in therapy is a memory; therefore, it can take you out of the present. Using grounding techniques to reassure yourself that you are present can help you manage your emotions when they feel overwhelming.

Practicing grounding techniques brings you to the here and now through your senses: sound, sight, touch, smell, and taste. You can practice these techniques inside the session with your therapist or outside the session.

DOPE EXERCISE: GROUNDING TECHNIQUES BY SENSE

SIGHT	SOUND	TASTE	SMELL	TOUCH
Play a game.	Call someone in your support system.	Eat your favorite food.	Use essential oils.	Hold ice.
Read a book.	Listen to the sounds around you.	Bite a lemon.	Light a candle.	Touch your hair or other parts of your body.
Label things you are looking at.	Play your favorite song.	Chew a piece of gum.	Take deep breaths.	Touch the ground outside.
Go for a walk and label what you see on your walk.		Grab your favorite Starbucks drink.		Touch a piece of fabric and focus on what it feels like.

I am a therapist who is trauma-informed, and I want you to be informed, too, so that you are able to understand what may be happening to you internally. Often it is our body's systems that are running the show, not the external world, and we don't always recognize that. What has happened to you is your experience. If you're comparing yourself to others and what they've gone through, you will always fall short of the true implications of trauma on your narrative. The reality is that it happened to you. The work on trauma starts by recognizing that you have experienced trauma. You can do this safely with a therapist who is trained to figure out what healing that trauma looks like for you.

DOPE TAKEAWAYS

» The brain can't distinguish the difference between a real or perceived threat when under stress.

» A trauma-informed therapist can recognize how trauma has impacted someone's life and may know some interventions. However, they aren't specifically trained in treating trauma.

» A trauma-trained therapist understands the impact of trauma and can navigate therapy sessions to process and use evidenced-based treatments to heal trauma.

» The amygdala alerts you that danger is near and can be overactive after trauma.

» Identifying trauma is the first step toward working on trauma.

CHAPTER NINE

FORGIVENESS

"Forgiveness is an inside job. Forgiveness, ultimately, is about freedom."

—NANCY COLIER

The healing journey can often get stuck at the forgiveness door: the door at the end of a dimly lit hallway, bolted shut. Behind that door is healing, accountability, joy, and survivor mentality. But in order to reach a healthier mental space, we first have to approach it. Your therapist can help you discover this door when pain from the past presents itself in the future, often through physical, mental, or emotionally charged reactions to a person, place, or thing.

You might have heard the phrase "forgiveness is for you" and wanted to give it the middle finger. We can often find ourselves resentful because it's not fair that we have to work on ourselves to reach forgiveness, especially when it's not always our fault that we are in pain. You are absolutely right; it is not fair. Your feelings are valid. You get to stay here as long as you would like.

When you're ready, approach the forgiveness door with your therapist. They will guide you through opening the door, climbing over what spills out, and walking through it. If you want to shut the door again at any time throughout this process, do it. The door is in your house and in your control. With your therapist by your side, turn on the hallway light and approach the forgiveness door.

There are three forms of forgiveness: 1) forgiving others for how they have treated you, 2) forgiving yourself for how you have treated others, and 3) forgiving yourself for how you've treated yourself. We are our own worst critics, and it's hard to recognize when we treat ourselves badly, especially if it's our default to think and talk about ourselves in a negative manner.

We don't have control over who hurts us, but we do have control over how we heal. Being a victim is not a choice. When you forgive, you take control over your narrative and make a conscious decision to release the strong emotions related to your pain. Healing is your responsibility.

WHAT IS FORGIVENESS?

"I want to forgive you, and I want to forget you." Lauren Conrad's line from *The Hills* has always stuck with me. Forgiveness is about choosing to let go of the emotions, such as sadness, anger, and fear, that keep you mentally caged and bound to your struggles. People aren't always deserving of your forgiveness, I know that. But forgiveness is not about letting people off the hook. They are still on the hook for what they did because you will remember; you don't ever forget what has happened to you. The person who hurt you may very well be living their life, and their best life at that. You deserve that too.

When you don't forgive, and instead hold on to the negative emotions associated with your pain, you risk mental exhaustion. Mental exhaustion can show up as ruminating thoughts: thoughts about feelings and negative experiences that are continuous. Ruminating thoughts can be triggered.

Let's say you recently applied for a job but were told you aren't a good fit for the company. After the interview, you start thinking about a previous relationship that ended when your partner cheated on you. You feel angry. You find yourself thinking that no one ever wants you. You go to bed angry and wake up feeling the same way. Over the next few days, you try to shake the emotions and negative thoughts associated with the trauma that the job rejection triggered. If you forgive your ex for cheating on you, you are not saying what they did was okay. Instead, you are releasing yourself from the anger. This decreases your chances of being triggered and experiencing ruminating thoughts. Future job rejections may remind you of your ex, but you won't find yourself continuously thinking about the negative experience with your ex. In *Atlas of the Heart*, Brené Brown writes, "Anger is a catalyst. Holding on to it will make us exhausted and sick. Internalizing anger will take away our joy and spirit; externalizing anger will make us less effective in our attempts to create change and forge connection. It's an emotion that we need to transform into something life-giving: courage, love, change, compassion, justice."

> When Yara was in middle school, the other girls would crack jokes about her being poor because she couldn't afford name-brand shoes. When she lands a job with a six-figure salary, she purchases her first pair of Louboutins. During one of her therapy sessions, her therapist compliments Yara's shoes. Yara doesn't acknowledge the compliment, and her therapist notices a change in Yara's body language. Her therapist asks if she has said something that changed Yara's mood. Yara processes being triggered to how she was made fun of for being poor in middle school. Having someone comment on her shoes, even in a positive way, makes her feel uncomfortable. She feels that people are making judgments about how much money she makes.
>
> "How can I consider forgiveness? The girls in middle school always reminded me I was poor; they basically made my life a living hell. I felt so embarrassed about my shoes and my life. If I could, I would have kicked their asses, but I feared suspension and my mother more than I did the bullying. I felt people were always judging what I wore, because of the bullying. I didn't know I was poor until someone else pointed it out," Yara says. "You also don't forgive yourself for not sticking up to them," her therapist reflects. "I guess not."

Yara's therapist found the forgiveness door. Yara struggled to forgive her bullies and to forgive herself. Working with her therapist, Yara starts to acknowledge her feelings toward the bullying in order to improve her self-esteem and overcome her resentment.

For Yara, the first step toward forgiveness is to acknowledge that she felt like a victim. To uncover what Yara feels she has lost, her therapist may have her retell her entire experience of being bullied, going back to the roots of "name it to tame it." You can't start the forgiveness journey without knowing the Who, What, and Why you are forgiving. The Who involves the people—the bullies and Yara herself. The What is related to the situation. In Yara's case, the What involves the other girls bullying her for being poor and herself for not standing up to them. And lastly, the Why. The Why stems from the emotions related to the Who and What. Yara struggles to receive compliments because she has low self-esteem after being bullied. In addition, she feels anger and resentment when her low self-esteem is triggered. Her Why may be that she wants to increase her self-esteem and release her feelings of anger.

For some, vengeance may be wanted and deserved. You want the person who hurt you to hurt like you did. However, vengeance is not always within our control or guaranteed. Waiting on something that is out of your control often prolongs your pain, and it doesn't always make the pain go away. However, you can gain control by choosing to release the feelings that led to wanting vengeance.

WHY SHOULD YOU FORGIVE?

Forgiveness does not mean that things will go back to the way they were. The truth is, you can't go back. I know, I know; this concept can suck. You may want to go back to who you were *before*. But you can't, and some acts of betrayal and hurt leave imprints that change our character and the way we move through life. Forgiveness will allow you to move toward figuring out who you want to be *after*.

> After working through the grief of losing my dog, an event that I wasn't prepared for resurfaced in my therapy sessions. There was a girl who went to my gym, and we would often chitchat between exercises. Struggling to create a supportive friend group after moving to Arizona, I decided to ask if she wanted to grab brunch. She said yes and I asked for her number. The bold extrovert in me texted her right away and said, "How about this weekend?" She responded with, "I can't

but how about another time?" "Perfect, how about next Saturday around 3 p.m.?" I texted. "Sure!" she responded.

The following Saturday came, and I did the usual check-in. "Are we still on for today?" Nothing. Absolute silence. This was unusual because we had been texting throughout the week and she always responded. However, I didn't think too much of it because emergencies happen. Two hours before we were supposed to meet, she texted me, "Sorry, I'm caught up doing housework." "Okay, when would be a good time to meet?" I asked. And then nothing. She never responded, and I felt so let down.

I brought up the situation in my therapy session on Monday, and to my surprise, I started crying. My feelings of being let down were actually disappointment and sadness. Turns out, I had been triggered by my unresolved feelings from my best friend ghosting me. I realized that without forgiving my best friend, I would stay stuck. If I didn't forgive him, I would continue to struggle when it came to being let down by others.

Your relationships will improve when you forgive. Now that you aren't carrying the baggage of anger, hate, and sadness, you may notice a shift in energy that allows you to show up in your relationships in a healthy way. That pain has made you resilient, and you've changed. You've changed into someone who isn't resentful. You may find yourself taking things less personally. You may start to notice that you start responding instead of reacting. You become more aware of the role you play in relationships and the purpose they serve.

Have you ever heard the quote "I am tired of being sick and tired"? Being in pain is physically, emotionally, and mentally draining and causes stress on the body. Stress is a silent killer, and forgiveness is like the support system to reducing stress. The forgiveness journey allows you to move into survivor mentality, where you're cognizant of accountability and you take care of yourself. When people and situations hurt you in the future, you're able to flex that mental muscle and identify your needs to meet them. By doing so, you protect yourself from stress, which will help improve your mental health.

Isn't that the point of all this work? To improve your mental health? Improving your mental health means reducing your symptoms. If you struggle with depression or PTSD, you may notice an improvement in symptoms as you learn to forgive. You may start to feel less anxious in situations or an increase in energy and functioning.

When you start to feel better, your confidence and self-esteem get an upgrade. Confidence is how you feel about your abilities, whereas self-esteem is how you feel about yourself. You may now feel less shame and guilt around the situation, leaving room to love yourself for the way that you are.

HOW FORGIVENESS CAN HELP YOU

Your mental health depends on forgiveness. It needs forgiveness. For different mental health conditions, such as anxiety and depression, your struggle to forgive can manifest in your fear that something bad may happen or your belief that you are not good enough.

We sometimes unconsciously internalize the things that occur in our external environment. We take what is happening and absorb it into our sense of self. Forgiveness can help you distinguish between your external world and you as a person so that you may place what has happened outside of yourself. Forgiveness allows you to understand that "this thing happened to me, but I am not the result of what happened."

When our self-worth is tied to what has happened to us, we can find ourselves not wanting to live. We want the pain to stop. A break from the mental exhaustion. The triggers to stop coming. We want to forget. And we can feel the only way to end the pain is to end our life. One of my supervisors, John, who is a featured Dope Expert in this book, once gave me a saying that I use with clients when they are feeling suicidal: "Something has to die off, and maybe that's not you." When you are hurting and want to escape the pain, the things that may need to die off are the feelings you harbor from something that has happened to you.

One benefit of letting go of resentment and anger is peace. Look at your pain as a broken bone. When you initially break your bone, you go to the doctor, and they give you a cast while you heal. The cast is therapy. After the cast is taken off, you may need some physical therapy to build strength and get back to using your leg. Forgiveness is like physical therapy. Although you may have started to heal the pain, forgiveness gives you the strength to move on.

Relationships with people are a part of being human. Working through what forgiveness looks like for you can help you in current and future relationships. Being resentful and holding grudges affects how you show up in your relationships. You may find that you struggle with trust or have a short temper and excessive irritability. The control and strength that you gain from forgiveness will allow empathy, compassion, and trust to flow in your relationships.

If you are waiting on an apology, know that you may never get one. Forgiveness lets the concept of an apology go. My parents used to say, "Don't hold your breath," and I never really understood what that meant until I started my healing journey. When you are waiting on an apology, you're essentially holding your mental breath. You're holding on to the idea that the person who hurt you is going to care about how they impacted you. In reality, they may not care. "Don't hold your breath" tells us not to wait, because otherwise you might just die waiting. I don't know about you, but I don't want to go out like that.

UNDERSTANDING THE IMPACT OF YOUR NARRATIVE

A narrative is a story you tell about the events that have happened in your life. Your narrative represents how you organize your world and creates meaning from events and experiences. Take a second to consider your narrative about something negative that has happened to you. Is it empowering to you? If not, how do you change your narrative?

The first step is to identify how your narrative makes you feel. When you are telling your narrative or thinking about the events, how do you feel? Anxious? Frustrated? Angry? Resentful? When I was a sophomore in college, my boyfriend of four years cheated on me. When people asked me why we broke up, I would say, "He cheated on me while I was in the hospital with my mom. And when I got back to our apartment, he had taken down all the pictures of us, and they were on the floor facing the wall." The way I told the story left me feeling angry, ashamed, and unworthy. It left me thinking, "Why me?"

After acknowledging how your narrative makes you feel, look for the problem outside of you. The problem was that someone I trusted had cheated on me. The problem was not that I wasn't enough. Sometimes we merge what has happened to us with negative thoughts. Thinking along the lines of "I was cheated on" made me feel like I wasn't enough. Instead, I had to shift my focus to "my ex cheated" to understand that him cheating had nothing to do with my worth. Him cheating was the problem, not me. Next, you want to identify the lesson.

> When I was in college, I was sexually assaulted while drunk by someone whom I had a crush on. For many years, I felt shame around the narrative because I later dated the person who assaulted me and because I didn't remember saying no. At the end of the night, intoxicated after several drinks, I passed out in the corner of my friend's living room. My crush started

kissing me and asking me to have sex. I don't specifically recall what I said, but I do remember trying to push him off me. Before I knew it, he had pulled my pants down and started having sex with me. I remember lying there and crying. My friend was asleep on the couch across the room, but they couldn't see because the room was dark. After my crush was done, I pulled my pants up, grabbed my phone, and went outside to call a friend of mine. When I called my friend, I interpreted what they said as, "What do you expect when you put yourself in these situations?" I woke up my other friend and asked if they could drive me back to my dorm. When they asked if it could wait until morning, I said no because I was just raped.

For many years, I told the story in a way that didn't serve me. I was ashamed of being drunk and taken advantage of. At the time, the idea of consent was mainly taught to girls, and it was modeled through verbal communication (saying the word "yes" or "no" out loud). Girls were often blamed for inviting unwanted attention because of how they dressed or carried themselves. I felt my story didn't fit the guidelines of sexual assault. One, I couldn't remember if I said no or not. Two, I was drunk. And three, I ended up dating the person some months later.

I have gained a better understanding of what it means to be a victim of sexual assault. Because I have a better understanding, I was able to forgive myself. I learned that you can withdraw consent at any time, that being drunk does not mean you deserved what happened, and that you can say no through body language, such as me pushing him. Forgiving myself has allowed me to stop being angry at my past circumstances, to not blame myself, and to hold the person who raped me accountable. It has allowed me to move from victim mentality to survivor mentality.

Now that I am in survivor mentality, my narrative looks different. The way that I tell my story doesn't make me feel ashamed.

"In college my crush took advantage of me while I was drunk. I said no by pushing him. He didn't listen." When you speak with survivor mentality, you place the blame where it is warranted. Survivor mentality also empowers you to adapt and change in ways that promote resiliency, to gain the power to overcome what has happened to you. You can create a new narrative of overcoming, surviving, and thriving. What happened to you doesn't define you.

HOW DO YOU FORGIVE?

You might be saying at this point, "Alright, alright, Shani! I get it, forgiveness is the way to go, but how the hell do I get there?" First, thank yourself. You want to thank yourself for getting yourself this far. Now, commit to changing your narrative, feelings, and thoughts. Holding on has protected you. It has played its role, and now it's time to hand that baton to the part of you that wants to experience life differently.

Let your narrative develop with your therapist. Allow them to guide you through the process of opening that door. If you find yourself holding back, communicate so your therapist can help you. Allow your therapist to help guide you as you label, identify, and clarify the meaning of your story.

As your narrative starts to develop, pay attention to how you are responding physically and emotionally. You may find it helpful to stop at certain parts, pause, and identify. Identify the people, situations, and feelings. The path to forgiveness requires identifying your emotions and identifying who hurt you. These are steps that cannot be skipped. If you aren't a talker, you can go through these steps in other ways. Ask your therapist if they have a sandbox, figures, or even drawing materials. Sometimes it may be helpful to physically draw your narrative and go from there.

Processing your narrative with your therapist may bring to light things that you weren't aware of. It's like having someone keep watch for safety concerns, gaps in the narrative, body language

WINDOW OF TOLERANCE

Hyperaroused State

- Fight/flight response
- Emotional reactivity
- Sweaty palms, increased heart rate
- Difficulty concentrating
- Panic, rage
- Hypervigilance

Optimal Level of Functioning

- Present, calm, and safe
- Can think and respond clearly
- Engaged and alert

Hypoaroused State

- Freeze response
- Lethargic, low energy
- Numb, lack of emotions
- Little to no physical movement
- Zoning out, dissociation
- Shut down

cues, and other aspects of your story that you may not have otherwise noticed. Your narrative can evoke feelings related to your pain that make you react physically. This is a normal part of the process that should be approached with the help of your therapist.

It's important to check in with your window of tolerance while processing. The window of tolerance is the sweet spot where you feel okay talking about heavy stuff in therapy. When you are within the window of tolerance, you are able to continue your narrative, take guidance from your therapist, and integrate information into tools outside of therapy. If you are outside of your window of tolerance, you can experience hyperarousal or hypoarousal.

Hyperarousal means that you are in flight-or-fight mode. Your body may want to flee as you feel overwhelmed and emotionally charged. *Hypoarousal* is the opposite. You may feel numb, find that you zone out, or want to shut down. While working with your therapist, you can expand your window of tolerance.

No matter what happens, remember your Why. Your Why is going to motivate you throughout the process. It may be helpful to use the statement, "I am working toward forgiveness because . . ." and fill in the blank. Write it down and stick that shit somewhere you can see every day as a reminder.

At some point, you should address how you will interact with yourself or the person who hurt you. That's right, boundary work! You may move through different stages of interaction. Maybe in the beginning you want no contact. As you start to make progress, you decide that you might want to start talking to them. You can choose to stay in contact, limit contact, or have no contact at all. Identifying how you want to interact with the person will decrease your chances of being emotionally charged or triggered while healing. Contact is not needed for forgiveness. No matter what you choose, please remember not to expect an apology. That takes the focus of forgiveness away from you. We are staying in control, owning our healing, and attempting to live our best f*ckin' lives! This is your forgiveness journey; there are no rules and no right or wrong ways to do it.

DOPE ACTION STEPS TOWARD FORGIVENESS

You know what forgiveness is, you know what the benefits are, and you know how to forgive. Now, let's talk tangible action steps. Forgiveness is not a linear process; it will look different for each person. Some of these suggestions may work, and others might not. You may need to tweak things to suit your unique situation. What matters is that you are taking action toward achieving your goals.

Practice gratitude. Gratitude is a part of positive psychology that focuses on being appreciative for the tangible and intangible things in your life. Practicing gratitude boosts your mood and improves emotional regulation. Best of all, gratitude can give you some resilience seeds to plant. Practicing gratitude is a tool that can be useful when adversity takes place in your life. If you can, practice gratitude daily.

DOPE EXERCISE: DAILY GRATITUDE PRACTICE

- *What was the highlight of your day today?*
- *What made you smile today?*
- *Who has supported you today?*
- *Identify a happy memory from your childhood.*
- *What positive change has come from attending therapy?*
- *What is a recent gift you received that made you happy?*
- *How are you fortunate?*
- *What is a positive change you recently made in your life?*
- *What are you thankful for about your job?*

DOPE EXERCISE: GRATITUDE FOR BLACK PEOPLE

- *What are you most proud about being Black?*
- *What do you love most about our culture?*
- *What is something you are thankful for about our history?*
- *What song from a Black artist makes you smile?*
- *Who is a Black person you admire and why?*
- *What social media accounts are a safe place for your Blackness?*
- *Where do you feel the safest as a Black person?*

Practice empathy. Empathy involves placing yourself in another person's situation. We have all hurt people, whether intentionally or unintentionally. I've done it and you've done it. When we practice empathy, we can be understanding of why people hurt people. Empathy does not mean saying, "It's okay." Instead, it means recognizing another person or yourself as someone who is human, and humans are fallible.

Grieve! Let the pain in. Identify what you lost. Was it your sense of safety? Your support system? Your self-esteem? Allow yourself to grieve that loss. Identify the stage of grief that you are in. There are five stages: denial, bargaining, anger, sadness, and acceptance. People assume that grief is only related to dying. Grief is about loss. The stages of grief are not linear. You may be feeling sadness one day and denial the next.

Find a release. Calm your thoughts. Journal, meditate, pray if you are spiritual—you do you. The purpose to these action steps is to calm the thoughts. Sometimes thoughts need a place to go outside of our heads. Some of these thoughts are about as annoying and intrusive as a telemarketer who keeps calling. But instead of avoiding the thoughts, give them an outlet. Let them live in the pages of your journal, or let your spiritual being take them on. Tell them thoughts, "Bye, Felicia."

Move your body. When you are struggling with forgiveness, move. Moving helps boosts your energy and mood.

Once you have learned forgiveness and can identify that you have forgiven, it's time to go back and retell your story. Sometimes, in retelling your story, you may notice that you haven't fully forgiven. You want your narrative to change along with you. Retelling your story will give you an insight into how you have changed. Your story is more than words; it includes your physiological reactions, emotions, and thoughts. Are you retelling your story from a survivor mentality? Does your story take accountability for your healing?

Today you commit to forgiving yourself and others. I'm hoping that if you take anything away from this book, it's this chapter. The essence of living a joyful life lies in our ability to forgive. Remember, the journey you are on is for *you*. Now, take a moment and hug yourself. Tell yourself, "I am working on forgiving. Please be patient with me."

DOPE TAKEAWAYS

» Forgiveness does not mean that you're saying what happened to you is okay.

» Forgiveness is taking responsibility and accountability for your life.

» The benefits to forgiveness are for you.

» Check in on your forgiveness process by retelling your narrative.

CHAPTER
TEN

INTERFERENCE WITH THERAPY

*"Under any circumstance, always do your best,
no more and no less."*

—DON MIGUEL RUIZ, *THE FOUR AGREEMENTS*

ometimes we stand in our own way. In life, standing in your own way doesn't always have severe side effects, but in therapy, the side effects can feel like a medication commercial. Just sitting there like, "Damn, if it has all those side effects, I'll just stay depressed."

Interference, or Therapy Interfering Behaviors (TIBs), are behaviors that can affect the outcome of therapy. They prevent you from successfully overcoming your problems and getting the most out of therapy. Not all TIBs are conscious and intentional. The term "interference" can have a negative connotation, so to prevent you from being too hard on yourself, let's look at TIBs as blind spots. The reality is that sometimes we aren't aware of the behaviors or even that they may be preventing growth. One of the main components of therapy is showing up. A part of showing up is owning behaviors that stand in your way.

NO-SHOWS AND CANCELLATIONS

Not showing up to therapy affects the therapeutic process. Recognizing what's preventing you from showing up will help you process how to overcome that issue. There can be many reasons for not showing up—maybe you don't feel ready, maybe you don't like your therapist, or maybe you have something more important to do. I am not here to judge you. I am here to raise awareness of behaviors that often prevent a client from completing their dope therapy journey.

Therapy is a process that works best through consistency. Growth and symptomatic relief in therapy are delayed when clients aren't consistent in showing up. Now don't get me wrong, life happens. But sometimes you have to ask yourself: "Is therapy a priority in my life?" It is okay for therapy to not be a priority. If so, you have to own that it may not be the right time for you to begin this process.

If you want to show up to the game of life and win, you have to practice. Therapy is your practice and scrimmage game. When you don't consistently practice for a sport, you don't learn how to get better at it. An athlete dedicates more time practicing to be better in the game. When you go to therapy, you are better equipped with the skills you require on the field of life.

DOPE EXERCISE: WHEN YOU SKIP A SESSION

Pause and ask yourself . . .

- *If I no-showed (instead of calling to cancel): Why didn't I want to call and cancel?*

- *Is what I did instead of going to therapy something that could have been rescheduled?*

- *Where does therapy rank in my priorities? List your top 5 priorities right now and label them 1 to 5 in order of importance, 1 being the most important.*

- *If therapy is in my top 5 priorities, what needs to change so that I can attend my appointments?*

I get that you might have jobs, kids, pets, or partners that can require you to shift your schedule at a moment's notice. Having a conversation with your therapist about the day and time of your appointment could be helpful to find what works best for you. Nowadays, most practices also offer telehealth, which allows for less drive time and better accessibility.

A random no-show or late cancellation can be viewed as a one-off. But consistently missing appointments or showing up late is a sign something in your life is interfering. It may be helpful to take a step back and label what is interfering with you attending your appointments on time. When we name it, we can tame it. Showing up late limits the time that you have to process. This can lead to sessions feeling rushed. Once you figure it out, or if you need help, you can approach the conversation with your therapist. Advocacy in the therapy room is a part of doing the work.

Self-advocacy is important in therapy because it helps you decide what you may or may not want. It also allows you to practice in a safe environment. Showing up late can affect not only you but also your therapist. In previous chapters, I mentioned how your therapist only gets paid for the time that you are present. If you use insurance and you show up even 10 minutes late, your therapist cannot bill for the full hour. We can only bill for face-to-face time. Let's say you have a 60-minute session at 11 a.m., but you arrive at 11:15 a.m. This leaves only 45 minutes for the appointment, which means your therapist can only bill for the 45-minute session. To hold you accountable or because they may have other clients, your therapist may not extend the session. This difference in billing time can severely impact a therapist's income. If the rate for a 45-minute session is $80 and the rate for a 60-minute session is $110, your therapist loses $30. So, if you see your therapist weekly and you show up late for a month, that is a total of $120 that your therapist won't be able to bill for. Existential psychiatrist Irvin Yalom states that one of our jobs as therapists is to teach empathy. It is my hope that by owning behaviors around late cancellations and no-shows, you will be more empathetic toward your therapist's time and schedule.

Arriving late can also affect the energy of the session. When you arrive late, this missed time can put a rushed feeling on the session. You may approach the session with the same intention of talking about everything but rush because you want to make sure you can fit it all in the time you have left.

DOPE EXERCISE: MEDITATION

Instead of focusing on the negatives of being called out around arriving on time, let's look inward to focus on the benefits.

1. *If you are in a safe place, close your eyes. Bring your attention to your breath, focusing on the inhale and exhale.*

2. *Notice if your tongue is placed on the roof of your mouth. If it is, let it fall and relax on the bottom of your mouth.*

3. *Now focus on being called out, and notice where you feel that. Is it in your chest? Is it in your shoulders? Is it in your back?*

4. *What emotions are associated with the physical feelings? Now would be a great time to refer to the list of emotions in Chapter 1.*

5. *Now breathe into the area of your body where you feel it, and when exhaling, open your mouth and release the negative energy. Breathe in ownership and accountability, and breathe out negativity and shame.*

MONTHLY SESSIONS

I'm not going to beat around the bush about monthly sessions. I do not believe in them unless a client is at the point of termination and it's a way to step down to see how they do. Monthly sessions, in my professional opinion, are not helpful. When a client only sees me monthly, we are playing catch up. That means that the client is catching me up on what has happened in the time between our sessions.

This interferes with therapy because too much time has elapsed for me to assess whether a client's symptoms have increased or decreased. There isn't enough time in the session to move from catch-up to process. In addition, clients on a monthly schedule usually have a hard time keeping up with homework, and will fall behind if they didn't understand it, if it is too hard, or if they're struggling to be consistent.

Monthly sessions prolong several processes: 1) rapport building, 2) development of significant change, and 3) moving from catching up to processing. To get the full benefit of therapy, there needs to be concentration, consistency, and rapport. Then there is canceling when you are on a monthly schedule. If a client needs to cancel or reschedule their appointment, that means there is even more time between sessions. I get that some people may be reading this and saying, "Well, Shani, isn't some therapy better than no therapy?" To an extent, yes; but when starting out, weekly or biweekly sessions are recommended, as monthly sessions interfere with progression.

VENTING IS NOT PROCESSING

Venting allows for emotionally charged energy to find a way out, and it can be good in some situations. But *just* venting in therapy can hinder progress. Now don't get me wrong, I am all for a good vent session with F-bombs flying around like confetti on New Year's, but it interferes with your growth if it is a reoccurring theme. The purpose of therapy is to assist you in areas of your life outside of the therapy room. If you are consistently venting, you and your therapist need to figure out how to move you into processing. Once you move into processing, you will label and identify your feelings, reflect on your thoughts about the situation, and gain clarification around the purpose of the event in your life. Venting is meant for the moment; it's not meant to be used in long-term processing with your therapist.

> Muranda has been feeling undervalued at her job. She got into the field of social work to help people like herself, but she notices that her employer only refers clients of color to her. She finds this to be hard because she wants to help people like her, but also wants to feel like her skills are being taken into consideration. She is not trained to work with families, but she

often gets referrals for family counseling. Muranda talks
extensively about her dissatisfaction with her employer in
therapy. Although Muranda started therapy to work on her
marriage, she finds that work comes up more and more. When
Muranda talks about her job, it is in a storytelling format that
recounts the day, and she often pushes back on open-ended
questions that require her to reflect on her feelings, thoughts,
and behaviors. Muranda leaves the sessions feeling like she got
something off her chest but with little to no insight into how the
situation impacts her emotionally and mentally.

Venting also can do the opposite of allowing for release. Sometimes just venting can actually increase your stress. Pause for a moment and think about a time in your life when you purely vented. How did you feel afterward? If you think about a time when someone upset you and then you vented to a friend, you might notice the original emotion returned. Are you familiar with the phrase "It's getting me upset just thinking about it"? With venting, even though you are not in the situation, you are rehashing it, and therefore reliving those original emotions.

According to Noam Shpancer, author of *The Good Psychologist*, processing in therapy means bringing past events or habits into our present consciousness and analyzing them using tools and knowledge to gain fresh insight. Venting stops at the point of consciousness, while processing takes it a step further by approaching the situations from the viewpoint of "What do I want to do with this?" When you process, you are able to identify behavioral changes that you would like to implement. Processing encourages your emotional and mental growth. And that's what you came to therapy for—growth.

A therapist's goal is to get you to a level of confidence in your abilities where you can take what you learn in the session and apply it to your life outside the sessions. If we are only coping with your issues in the session, you aren't implementing skills in the areas of your life where you can benefit. If this continues to happen, you may find your therapy journey prolonged. Yes, you are talking about it in therapy, but you aren't doing anything about it in your life. What happens outside the therapy sessions is a part of how your goals are measured. You may then find yourself feeling like therapy isn't working if nothing is changing outside the sessions.

The game changer for processing is when healthy coping skills are developed. When you are talking in therapy, your therapist will assist you in identifying, clarifying, and labeling your feelings, thoughts, and behaviors. During this process we can find areas of your life where coping skills are needed.

DOPE EXERCISE: HOW TO FIGURE OUT YOUR COPING SKILLS

- *Create a therapy notebook. This notebook is only to be used during your therapy process.*
- *At the end of every session, journal about what you discussed and name at least two takeaways from the session that can help with the situation you processed in therapy.*
- *Practice at least one coping skill between sessions.*
- *Journal how it went when you practiced the coping skill.*
- *Discuss with your therapist how your coping skill went.*

EXAMPLES OF HEALTHY COPING SKILLS

- *Meditation*
- *Twerking*
- *Exercising*
- *Talking to a supportive friend*

- *Taking a nap*
- *Journaling*
- *Cooking*
- *Spending time alone*
- *Reading a book*
- *Taking part in an activity that brings humor (seeing a comedy show, laughing with friends)*
- *If you are spiritual, going to church*
- *If you are spiritual, praying*
- *Making an extra therapy appointment when you need it*
- *Hiring a career coach to help with career challenges*
- *Listening to music*
- *Practicing writing three things you are grateful for daily*

AVOIDANCE

Avoidance can show up in many ways. We can avoid the session, the topic, or the emotions related to a topic. Avoidance tells us something about our emotional state and our bodies. A small gesture of avoidance can look like the loss of eye contact or a sudden shift in tone or body language. Or it could look like a client saying, "Yeah, I'm good. I don't want to talk about that." Avoidance can show up as a maladaptive coping mechanism or a defense mechanism. Defense mechanisms are unconscious psychological strategies that protect us from unwanted thoughts and feelings. Maladaptive coping skills are skills that do not help us sit in difficult emotions and thoughts. Avoidance is a temporary fix, not a long-term solution. Prior to therapy, you may have been in situations where you had to avoid in order to survive. This can replay itself in the therapy room. Your therapist will be able to help you identify which one it is.

DEFENSE MECHANISM	WHAT IT IS	EXAMPLE
Denial	A refusal to accept reality. We block things from our mind so that we don't have to deal with them.	Someone who refuses to see the signs of their partner's infidelity.
Projection	Attributing unwanted thoughts, feelings, and motives to another person.	Someone may dislike their friend's friend, but instead of acknowledging it, they tell themselves that the friend doesn't like them.
Repression	Unconsciously hiding thoughts and feelings from the conscious mind. (This doesn't mean they don't exist, as they may still show up in behaviors.)	Someone was bitten by a dog as a child and is now afraid of dogs. They repress the memory and struggle to explain why they are afraid of dogs as an adult.
Displacement	Directing strong emotions and frustrations onto a powerless target.	Someone had a rough day at work and comes home and yells at their partner.
Regression	Escaping to an earlier time of safety when feeling threatened.	After moving in with their partner, someone goes back to their parents' house to stay after an argument.
Rationalization	Using your own facts to explain something that is undesirable or to make something less threatening.	When something bad happens and people say, "Everything happens for a reason."

DEFENSE MECHANISM	WHAT IT IS	EXAMPLE
Sublimation	Directing unacceptable emotions onto something that is appropriate and safe.	When someone is angry, they go to a smash room (a business that allows you to smash things with a sledgehammer).
Reaction formation	When you recognize how you feel but you behave in the opposite manner.	Someone who is angered by the diversity inclusion meeting but acts overly positive.

We might often think that avoidance is a great way to manage stress. But the reality is that stress doesn't go away; it just shifts into another feeling. I want you to think of the emotions that you feel as energy. According to the Law of Conservation of Energy, energy can neither be created nor destroyed, only converted. When you feel angry and happy, your emotions are still energy, just converted differently. When you use avoidance to deal with stress, your stress never goes away; its energy just shifts. Although you may not be acknowledging the stress, it is still there.

You may have learned avoidance as a child—a lot can go back to childhood. Growing up in a Black family, if I asked my mother "why" I was told, "Don't talk back." I learned to avoid asking questions as a defense mechanism. We only know what we know. If you avoid feelings, topics, or even therapy sessions, it keeps you stagnant. Maybe you're frustrated that therapy isn't working or you're frustrated that your therapist keeps inquiring about something you don't want to talk about. Avoidance doesn't solve anything, and what you are struggling with can potentially increase. What you resist, persists.

Now, I am not saying that you have to divulge when your therapist asks about things you'd rather avoid. I am saying to be open to the conversation about how this avoidance has developed and why you employ it.

> Muranda often gets frustrated when her husband doesn't take out the trash. She will ask, but she usually ends up taking it out herself at the end of night. She avoids talking about the garbage by continuing to just take it out. One morning while making breakfast, she finds that there are no eggs. She becomes bitter. Eggs had been on the shopping list she had sent with her husband to the store. Muranda finds herself feeling edgy and flips out on her husband, yelling about how he never does anything she asks. Not having eggs is merely a smaller issue that's being compounded with her avoidance of the trash issue. But in the heat of the moment, it seems like her anger is only about the eggs. Avoiding talking about the garbage has left her feeling vexed; the avoidance was only a temporary fix.

When this behavior shows up in the therapy room, it can halt progress. Your therapist may referee avoidance with an empathetic approach. This approach can prevent you from feeling shame. Instead, your therapist wants to bring attention to what is preventing your progress. A great place to start is by communicating the meaning of avoidance in your life to your therapist. Avoidance can show up during therapy in a few ways. Do you . . .

- Avoid questions asked by the therapist?
- Avoid a particular topic?
- Avoid an emotion?
- Avoid responsibility in a situation you're describing to process in the session?

When your therapist does or says something that bothers you, I encourage you to bring it up. It's more harmful than helpful if things remain unaddressed in any relationship. Avoidance in therapy sessions is a TIB because it has the potential to lead you to avoid therapy altogether. As humans, we often take negative experiences and apply them to all other scenarios that mimic the original experience. The brain sometimes struggles to tell real from fake, and because of this, if you have a negative experience with a therapist, you may think all therapists are that way. Let's take a look at an interaction between Joshua and his therapist.

> **Therapist:** Joshua, you appear to be frustrated today. Is that how you're feeling?
>
> **Joshua:** Obviously.
>
> **Therapist:** Would you like to talk about your frustration?
>
> **Joshua:** I feel you have this expectation for me to be cheerful and positive.
>
> **Therapist:** That's an expectation you feel I have of you?
>
> **Joshua:** I mean, yeah. Otherwise why would you ask?! *grunts*
>
> **Therapist:** The upset and frustration seems to have shifted to me.
>
> **Joshua:** Sorta!!!
>
> **Therapist:** Me calling out your frustration, did that frustrate you even more?
>
> **Joshua:** Yeah, but I'm not sure why.
>
> **Therapist:** Could it have been the way I said it?
>
> **Joshua:** Naw, that's not it.
>
> **Therapist:** Take a beat. Where in the conversation did I start to frustrate you?

Now I am not justifying all the mistakes therapists can make. What I am suggesting is that you consider how you might handle the situation if your therapist says something you're not okay with. Is there a possibility that you can use the opportunity to practice advocating for yourself and see if it is possible to work through it? Your therapist responded in a way you don't like? Address that shit. Your therapist constantly shows up late? Address that shit. The beauty in it is that, because of our profession, therapists are usually receptive to feedback. This may be a great opportunity to revisit the discussion of conflict in Chapter 5.

The desire to be liked by your therapist can sometimes supersede the truth in your narrative. Of course, we want to vibe with our therapist on a level that allows us to show up in the mess that we are sometimes. However, this can interfere with therapy. Because you want your therapist to like you, you may omit details that make you look bad. Yes, therapists have their own ways of viewing the world, but our job is to remain objective and be on the same page with you instead of judging you.

> In a recent therapy session, Quinn focused on processing their recent one-night stand and the guilt they felt as a result of it. But they omitted a key detail from their narrative when talking to their therapist. Quinn was feeling guilty because the one-night stand was with their ex. Instead of telling their therapist this, Quinn deflected and attributed their guilt to being at odds with their values.

Leaving out details of your narrative detracts from the credibility of a process that allows you to be seen while working through it. You may omit details due to shame or because you feel like you have discussed a part of your life a little too much. It's your life and what you are dealing with, so it's relevant to therapy. If you need to process it over and over to gain further clarity and insight, that's okay. (PS You can never discuss something too much in therapy.)

NO EXCUSES

Therapists hear many excuses related to therapy. "I can't afford it," "I don't have time," "I don't really NEED therapy," "I tried it and the therapist sucked." Yes, all of these reasons are excuses. I do not mean to invalidate you, but we have to take a look at the risk of your excuses.

Excuses keep you comfortable. Let's look at "I can't afford therapy." This is where we can revisit Chapter 2. There are many services available to be able to make therapy affordable in some areas, such as sliding-fee scales, community resources, grants, scholarships, and more. If we can reframe "I can't afford it" to "I am looking into a way to afford therapy," you leave room for possibilities without shutting the idea down completely. If we are being honest, and this is coming from someone who has lived paycheck to paycheck, *we find a way to afford the things we want, even if they aren't always the things we need.*

Speaking of things that we need, it is necessary to do homework outside of the session. I wanted to reiterate how important homework is. When you don't do the homework, you don't learn what does or does not work for you in your life. Homework is a way for you to practice and strengthen your skills outside the therapy room. If there is nothing to report back on, sessions can be lots of processing with no action. When there is no action, there is little behavioral change. Know that homework doesn't always mean completing the assignment, but putting in the effort is crucial.

Say you have anxiety around coffee shops and your homework is to go to a small coffee shop. You get into your car, drive to the coffee shop, and sit in your car in the parking lot . . . but you never go in. You have still completed your homework. You're probably wondering: How? Because you put in the effort. And now you can talk about the feelings and thoughts you had sitting in that parking lot during your next therapy session. And, of course, we are going to take the statement "I didn't complete the homework assignment" and say, "I made an attempt to go inside, which I am proud of because I realized I can do things."

Stop reading for a moment and hug yourself. Repeat the following:

I am not defined by my actions.

I am choosing the therapy journey because I recognize that I am capable of thriving in life. (Say your name), therapy can feel hard and challenging at times, but I am doing it.

I am here, I am strong, and I refuse to stand in my own way.

I ask that I please step aside, so I can thrive.

Now squeeze yourself tight and say, "My therapy journey is dope and so am I." Please remember to be kind to yourself on this journey. I believe in you. I know therapy can feel overwhelming and defeating at times. Honestly, most people interfere with their therapy process without even knowing they are doing it.

If you recognize that you have been interfering in your therapy process, you might not change overnight. But that is not the expectation. The expectation is awareness—to be aware of how your behaviors are hindering your growth. You can then choose to either continue with the TIBs or work on them. This is one of the few moments in your life when you don't have to work on it alone; you get a dope-a$$ therapist who calls you out on your sh*t from a caring place. You get to understand why you're interfering with therapy and how this can show up in other areas of your life. I guarantee that if they are interfering with your therapy, these same behaviors are also interfering somewhere else in your life.

I've discussed how therapy mimics real life. Your relationships outside of therapy are visible in your relationship with your therapist. The behaviors you express in therapy are behaviors that are expressed outside of therapy. Unlearning can be a challenging part of therapy. You are the way you are through learned and lived experiences; own that. But now, you get to step aside from who you are to become who you want to be.

DOPE TAKEAWAYS

» Therapy Interfering Behaviors (TIBs) can be intentional and unintentional.

» TIBs affect your growth in the therapy process, which is why attention is brought to them.

» Venting is just talking, but processing is analyzing and using tools that provide different insights so that you may take action toward change.

» Avoidance is an unhealthy maladaptive coping skill that does not allow you to process your emotions and thoughts.

» Excuses hinder the process because they prevent you from owning your actions.

CHAPTER ELEVEN

11

IS THERAPY HELPING?

"The only time we should look back to yesterday is to look at the positive things that were accomplished to encourage us to do better things today and tomorrow."

—STEVIE WONDER

||| 'm that bish who will go to the gym for 60 minutes, spend most of her time dancing to K CAMP's "Comfortable," do 30 minutes of ab work and 30 minutes of bench-pressing, then lift up my shirt and ask, "Where the hell are my abs?" I need to know that the time and investment I'm putting into getting up early and going to the gym is going to give me abs. Most of the time, I end up thinking that the gym is not giving what it's supposed to give. And then, later that night when I'm dancing to Christina Aguilera's "Dirty," naked and waiting for the shower to heat up, I'll catch a glimpse of my arm and think, "Oh shit . . . it's working." So, I'll get up and go to the gym again the next day.

Sometimes you might not be aware of how therapy is impacting your life. You have goals that you want to attain and may not be paying attention to the small steps it takes to get there. Knowing that therapy is working will help motivate you to keep going. Therapy is an investment of energy, finances, and time, and you want a return on that investment.

When you start attending therapy, you create goals with your therapist. Goals in therapy should be realistic and attainable, and it is your therapist's job to ensure that they are. One way to know if therapy is working is by checking in on the progress toward your goals. For example, if your goal is to improve your self-esteem, you would want to clarify what higher self-esteem would potentially look like for you and how you will know when you have achieved your goal. You have clarified that high self-esteem looks like feeling good about the things you wear and not caring what anyone else thinks. After clarifying, you can start to measure small changes that may be hinting at an increase in your self-esteem. Maybe you recently received a compliment and just said thank you instead of explaining where you got the outfit from. Accepting the compliment instead of brushing it off is a small step toward your larger goal.

Therapy isn't always in the tangible action steps; sometimes it is in the uncovering. If you are coming to therapy because you are unhappy, therapy can help you uncover the source of the unhappiness. Once you uncover the source, you can work on problem-solving. Proceeding without uncovering the source is like putting duct tape on a leak. Yes, it fixes the problem temporarily. But because we haven't found the source of the leak, the duct tape will eventually fall off and the faucet will continue to leak.

TRACKING YOUR SYMPTOMS

One of the things you can pay attention to is whether your symptoms have improved. You'll first need to identify what your symptoms are. Take a look at what you are struggling with. This could be sleep, appetite, mood, or energy—anything that prevents you from functioning in the way that you want to.

From here, you can use your symptoms to measure your improvement. Say you are struggling with sleeping, so you first identify how many hours of sleep you get a night. That way, when you are in therapy and working toward improved sleep, you now have something to log your improvement against. Improved sleep will be your sign that therapy is helping.

You may have days when your symptoms feel or look worse. That is a normal part of the process. In addition to logging the day-to-day changes, pay attention to how you feel overall. Life happens. Maybe you stayed up late the last few nights to finish writing a paper and didn't get much sleep. But on other nights throughout the week, you went to bed on time and got restful sleep. Outside of this one-off situation, you have been improving your sleep routine.

Tracking your symptoms can be done in your therapy journal. In the beginning, you should track them daily. Try assigning your symptoms a severity level using a numeric scale. For example, on a scale of 1 to 5, 1 could be no irritability and 5 could be the worst irritability you've ever felt. Or you use a simple yes or no measurement, where you can either say, "Yes, I felt irritable today" or "No, I didn't feel irritable." If you don't want to keep a journal, your therapist may have a log tool for you to use.

DOPE EXERCISE: TRACKING YOUR SYMPTOMS

When you begin therapy, choose three symptoms that you would like to improve and track them daily in your therapy journal.

- *Keep a daily log of whether you experienced each symptom.*
- *Write about what happened right before you experienced your symptom.*
- *Write down if you used a coping skill and label whether it was helpful.*
- *At the end of each week, tally up how many times you experienced each symptom.*
- *Pay attention to weekly trends as well as the day-to-day.*

Quinn has been working with their therapist to create attainable and measurable goals around their sleep and irritability. Prior to therapy, Quinn would sleep three to four hours a night. Most days, Quinn felt irritable and angry with people they came in contact with. They set two goals: 1) to sleep seven hours a night and 2) to feel less irritated. Quinn's therapist encourages them to track their irritability throughout the day. They write down when they are irritated and identify the cause. They notice that they felt most irritated when a white person tries to touch their locs and when their twin calls them to complain. In sessions, Quinn discusses their nightmares around being a Black person in America and their thoughts of being pulled over by a white police officer, and after asking if they can get their wallet out of their back pocket, getting shot while reaching for it.

Around the three-month mark, Quinn becomes frustrated with therapy. They don't feel any improvement. Quinn still has nightmares and still feels irritable. Their therapist points out that in the previous session, Quinn had talked about sleeping roughly five hours a night and had nightmares less frequently. "But they aren't gone!" Quinn exclaims in frustration. "That's the end goal. If we step back and measure your steps toward the end goal, we are on track," their therapist responds. Quinn has never looked at it this way. They had been measuring success in therapy as achieving the overall goal. Looking at the small improvements helped them understand that therapy is working.

Much of therapy is about processing *why* you have the symptoms that you have. Learning why you struggle to be social, sleep, or control eating habits is a large part of therapy. Quinn struggled to sleep because they were having nightmares. If the therapist jumped into trying to fix Quinn's sleep problems without addressing why the nightmares were occurring, Quinn wouldn't learn how to cope and manage their symptoms better.

This is why psychiatrists often recommend that clients on medications are also in therapy. The medications can help relieve the symptoms but don't fix why they occur. Symptom improvement is a sign that therapy is helping, but we have to push through to understand and cope with why they have manifested so that therapy can be successful.

You're on the right track when you start using coping skills to manage your symptoms. Quinn learned that their nightmares are more intense when they scroll through social media before bed due to seeing posts about past murders of Black people by cops. They decide to limit their intake of these kind of stories and put away their phone an hour before bed. This puts a limit on how much information they are digesting related to this topic and allows them to get into a more relaxed state before sleep.

INCREASED INSIGHT AND AWARENESS

Insight is understanding the cause and effect of your past behaviors, thoughts, feelings, and relationship patterns: the why, what, how, who, and when. Awareness is consciously applying this insight into your day-to-day behaviors and reactions. Awareness is a part of the process of responding, of noticing your thoughts and behaviors in the moment and being able to act on them. When you start identifying your feelings in the moment, you become aware of how situations impact you and can choose how to respond. Now you have a choice, and having a choice is empowering and feels hella good!

When you have a greater understanding of why you do what you do, you can change. When you know better, you do better. Let's say you have had a pattern of unsuccessful relationships. You came to therapy to get insight into how you show up in relationships to increase the chances that your next relationship will be successful and healthy.

In therapy you learn about your anxious attachment style. You also dive into the manifestation of your attachment. In learning about your attachment style, you gain the skills necessary to form a secure relationship. You now know that in order to feel more secure in relationships, your anxious attachment style needs healing. In addition, you learn how to identify your needs and wants so that you are able to effectively communicate them to your potential partner. Now that you better understand why your previous relationships may have failed, you will be better able to identify your needs and wants in future relationships.

THE TRANSTHEORETICAL MODEL

You are going to therapy because you want to make changes. This is an intentional decision. The transtheoretical model (TTM), developed by James Prochaska and Carlo DiClemente, conceptualizes the process of making intentional changes.

According to the model, there are six stages to change: precontemplation, contemplation, preparation (or determination), action, maintenance, and relapse (or recycling). You can apply the model to assess whether therapy is helping you create change.

STAGE	WHAT IT MEANS	APPLIED	STRATEGIES
1. Precontemplation	You are unaware of the need to change and have no plans to take action in the future. You don't recognize the pros of changing.	"I work 50-plus hours a week, which is the norm."	What are the risks if you don't change?
2. Contemplation	You have intention to change but are weighing the pros and cons. You may still feel ambivalent.	"I only get four hours of sleep a night, and I'm really tired. I should do something about this."	Make a pros and cons list. What barriers may get in the way of change?
3. Preparation (or determination)	You are ready for action. You may take small steps. You believe in the change you are making.	"I need to set boundaries around my work schedule. I set an alarm to stop working at 5 p.m."	Identify your goals and write them down. Have 2–3 affirmations that are related to your goal. What is your plan to change?

STAGE	WHAT IT MEANS	APPLIED	STRATEGIES
4. Action	You're doing it! You're putting in work to change your behavior (using coping skills, responding instead of reacting, etc.).	"I have a boundary that I won't work more than nine hours a day. I now have more time with friends and family, and I feel less tired."	Reward, reward, reward!!! Seek an accountability partner.
5. Maintenance	You have sustained your changed behavior and work to prevent going back to old behaviors.	"I set a boundary around going out during the week so I make it to bed on time. I feel more energized."	Reward, reward. What coping skills can you use if you find yourself wanting to return to old behaviors?
6. Relapse (or recycling)	You have a setback to older behaviors.	"My boss scheduled meetings past my boundary, and instead of addressing it, I let it go. I feel exhausted today."	What were the triggers? Remember your Why.

As you are working toward creating change, it helps to identify what stage of change you are in. What were some behaviors prior to entering therapy that you wanted to change? Identify two to three of them. For example, maybe you felt anxious whenever you were in the room with your mother. You didn't like feeling this way and you wanted things to change. In therapy, you processed that you worry your mom will bring up politics and having this type of conversation with your mother increases your anxiety. Your therapist encourages you to implement a boundary with your mom, which is the action stage of the model. Now you have a boundary in place that you don't talk politics with your mom, which has decreased your feeling of anxiety. By taking action and making change, you proved to yourself that therapy is helping.

Moving through the stages is another indicator that therapy is working, even if you have a setback to old behaviors. When this happens, I find it helpful to have clients pause and look back. There are times when this is helpful, unlike in scary movies. We feel failure and defeat because we are looking ahead at the end game. But, if you stop and look behind you to see how far you've come, you can realize that it's not a setback; it's just a moment of pause to reshift.

DOPE EXERCISE: DEALING WITH A SETBACK

If you have a setback, ask yourself . . .

- *What can this setback teach me?*

- *What do I need to do to get back to the action stage?*

- *What am I feeling?*

- *What would be helpful to bring into my therapy sessions to help progress forward?*

IMPLEMENTING TOOLS

I don't want you thinking that therapy is only working when you can see change and action. It's about finding your baseline prior to therapy and then comparing it to where you are now.

In therapy, you will learn many tools to apply to your life. When you go from contemplating a tool to implementing it, you know that therapy is doing its job—especially when you start to behave, think, and feel differently. To start practicing skills, we first need to get you the right tools: tools for you, tools for others, tools for your mind, tools for your emotions; *in my Oprah voice* everything gets a tool!

There are tools that your therapist uses and then there are tools that you use. Your therapist's tools consist of their approach, interventions, and resources. We have to figure out what the issue is and what is causing the issue. If you have been feeling anxious when you wake up, breath work may be a helpful tool to help you feel calm in the immediate moment. However, we also need to know why you are feeling anxious when you wake up. As an approach to figuring out the issue, your therapist may have you walk them through a typical evening before you go to bed. Then they may want to know what your anxiety feels like by having you describe it physically. Having you clarify is the intervention. If you tell them that you have heavy breathing, guiding you through breath work is also an intervention. Your therapist might recommend resources by suggesting some good books about anxiety.

Once your therapist finds out why, they now have the information to choose a tool for you to implement. It's important to ask questions when your therapist gives you tools. For example: "How will this help me?" "Why have you chosen this tool for me?" "Can you show me how it works?" Implementing tools can be a process of trial and error. Sometimes you and your therapist might find that a tool doesn't work as desired. If this happens, you and your therapist will go back to further clarify the issue. That is why when you begin to implement the recommended tool, your therapist will inquire about your experience.

When you start coping with things differently, you're using tools to take care of your physical, mental, and emotional well-being. If you struggled to cope when shit hit the fan prior to therapy and you now find yourself calming down quicker than usual and problem-solving, you're growing in therapy.

SETTING AND EVALUATING GOALS

At the beginning, you and your therapist should have developed some goals for therapy. Goals give you an insight into how and why you're investing in your mental health journey. It's okay if you started therapy with only the intention of wanting to feel better. But as you make progress in therapy, you may find that you have to shift your goals. You might have started therapy with the intention of wanting to alleviate symptoms of depression and decrease self-harm. Once you are feeling better, you may find that your goals shift and become more introspective as you gain clarity. Shifting goals is a sign that growth is happening. It means that you are becoming more insightful and aware of what direction you want to go for your therapy journey.

How do you create goals? Start by answering: "Why am I coming to therapy?" Write down all the reasons that you want to attend therapy, big or small. Let the words flow. Then, look through your list and see if any themes are visible. Now that you have identified a few things that you want to work on, get more specific. Being specific guides us in the direction of making attainable and measurable goals. Lastly, consider the timeline of your goal. It's sometimes hard to put a time on therapy goals, but a time stamp can be used as a check-in. You and your therapist can then assess if the goals are achievable and relevant.

For instance, if you say that you want to be happy, your therapist will guide you to think about this deeper. Why do you want to be happy? What does happiness look like for you? What are you currently struggling with that is making you unhappy? You specify that you want to find ways to cope with your stress at home so that you're less irritable.

Next, you will target what makes you irritable. To make an attainable goal, we have to identify the causes. Once the causes are identified, you and your therapist will work to see what is within your control to alleviate irritability. During this process, you will label your emotions and clarify why you feel irritable and what you may have already tried. Then a goal will be made using a tool to assist in alleviating your irritability. Your therapist will check in to see if the tool is working and if you're starting to meet the goal of feeling happy. The catch here is that you may alleviate the irritability but not be happy. When this happens, the expectation around the goal may need more defining.

WHAT IF I FEEL WORSE?

You came to therapy to feel better, so feeling worse can make you feel like something is not right. But the saying is true; it may get worse before it gets better. To explain this phenomenon, we have to bring grief into the conversation.

When you are in the process of changing, you may start to grieve your old self. With change comes loss. Working with your therapist to identify the loss is essential to understanding why it feels worse. As much as you may want to change, there can be parts of you that are in denial about whether the change is beneficial. You may also feel angry that you have to do the work to change.

Sometimes you feel worse due to resistance. You are fighting the change that needs to occur. Although shit sucks, you at least know what to expect. You don't know what it's like to change. You know sadness and pain, but you don't know happiness and joy. As you are changing, figuring out the new transition may feel foreign. You may feel displaced, which encourages your resistance.

The work in therapy requires you to unlearn, and then learn new ways to navigate life, identify your emotions, respond to situations, and interact in your interpersonal relationships. This can feel overwhelming at times. Processing in therapy is a different way of thinking about your struggles. You are expressing your emotions and being open in ways that you weren't before. Your defense mechanisms are being broken down, and you can't hide behind them anymore. In order to become the person that you want to be, you must fully see and understand the person that you are. Tapping into painful memories, retelling stories, and rehashing emotions can make things worse. In order to grow, we must recognize and change the things that prevented you from healing. If at any point you feel you can't handle something, communicate to your therapist and support team.

DOPE EXERCISE: HOW TO DEAL WHEN IT FEELS WORSE

- *Speak up. Consistently communicate with your therapist about how you are feeling throughout the process.*
- *Create a buffer after sessions. Give yourself a minimum of 15 minutes to decompress after sessions.*
- *Remind yourself that you have gotten you this far and you can take yourself further.*
- *Check in with your sense of security.*
- *Identify a support person whom you can call if your therapist is not available.*
- *Identify the local crisis line and save their number in case you need it.*
- *Move your body.*

WHY THERAPY MIGHT NOT BE WORKING

If you're in therapy and thinking, "I feel like this isn't helping," you need to talk about therapy in therapy. There are many reasons why therapy may not be working; it could be an entirely separate book. If you feel like therapy isn't working and you aren't sure why, talk to your therapist. Speak up and let them know how you are feeling about the process. You and your therapist should be having check-ins about where you are in the process, how far you've come, and where you are going.

You might find that therapy isn't working because your therapist isn't the right therapist for you. You need to feel like your therapist and their approach are helping you. If you don't feel that your therapist is helping you, talk about it. Maybe the way your therapist approaches therapy isn't helpful for your struggles, and you need a different modality. Maybe your therapist draws their approaches from Existential Therapy, but you are in need of Dialectical Behavioral Therapy. Your therapist can then either switch up their approach if they are trained or refer you to someone else.

Are you holding back? The work of therapy cannot authentically take place if you are holding back. If you are holding back, ask yourself why. This may mean revisiting Chapter 10 to figure out if there are any factors preventing you from getting what you want out of therapy.

~~~~~~

DOPE EXERCISE: HOW TO KNOW IF THERAPY IS WORKING

If you're unsure whether therapy is working, as yourself these questions.

- *Am I feeling hopeful?*
- *Am I identifying my emotions?*
- *Am I pausing to choose a response?*
- *Am I thinking and feeling differently?*
- *Do I take risks to implement new tools?*

- *What stage of change am I in?*
- *Do I feel that my therapist is helping me?*
- *Do I feel resilient, like I have the ability to bounce back?*

DOPE EXPERT: KRISTA JORGENSEN MA, LPCC
(www.numapsychotherapy.com)

Krista Jorgensen owns and operates a group private practice in Minneapolis. She works primarily with people who have borderline personality disorder, trauma, attachment disorders, and LGBTQ+ issues. Her positive intention shines as a therapist in the therapy room. I thought we would get her feedback to help gain further clarity in understanding how to tell if therapy is working.

Krista, can you shine some light on understanding how someone can distinguish between feeling like therapy is working and/or if therapy has come to an end?

Discontinuing therapy should be a collaborative process between client and therapist. If therapy is working, the client should be seeing progress in meeting their treatment goals. Clients may notice they're feeling better and having an easier time managing stressors. It can be difficult to discern if therapy is working or if it's time to end.

I continue working with clients to solidify gains and new skills until they feel those skills are well integrated. Once this has happened, it's often time to end therapy. To maintain long-term progress, it may be important to make follow-up appointments as needed.

But what if it's not working? How can someone in therapy approach this?

Directly and honestly! Therapists are responsible for managing their own emotions around their effectiveness. While therapists are experts in mental health, clients are the experts in their own lives and experiences.

~~~~~~

Y'all, she took us back to the roots of a healthy therapeutic relationship—the client and therapist communicating honestly about what is and is not working. Krista reiterated that, due to the relational nature of therapy, therapists want to hear your feedback. In fact, they are trained to take in and apply feedback, so approach your therapist directly and honestly.

Krista further emphasizes that when therapy is not working, it may correlate to the attachment and relational concerns you are coming into therapy to address. If you don't want to talk about your feeling that therapy is not working with your therapist, it may be a sign that you need a new therapist.

Being in a place where you look forward to seeing your therapist and being in therapy is a good sign. Having that my-therapist-gets-me feeling means that you are opening up so that someone can see you. It means that you are putting in the effort and work. Looking forward to the sessions is also an indicator that you are motivated to change. This good feeling may come and go, so capitalizing on it when it's there can be helpful.

You get out what you put in. Therapy isn't meant to be forever, but its work is meant to stay with your forever. Paying attention to your day-to-day, week-to-week, and month-to-month allows you to get a greater sense of who you are becoming. Don't let the small setbacks defeat you. Let the small successes carry you. If you feel exhausted by the process, it's okay to take a break or switch gears. There is no right way to do therapy. Its success is dependent upon you. Go bad bish, go bad bish, go!

DOPE TAKEAWAYS

» Use a therapy journal to track symptoms and how you are feeling about the therapy process.

» Tracking your symptoms helps you know if therapy is helping.

» If a tool isn't working, check in with your therapist.

» Talk to your therapist to have a better understanding of whether therapy is working for you.

CHAPTER
TWELVE

CLOSURE

"It's more about remembering rather than getting over or saying goodbye."

—JOHN JANKORD MA, LMFT, LADC, LPCC

hen the goals established at the beginning have been achieved and the therapist and client mutually agree on ending, therapy has run its course. That's a healthy goodbye.

Goodbyes aren't always traditional in therapy, a space where you come in, have goals for treatment, complete the goals, and then say deuces. There are many reasons that may lead you to end your therapy journey. Throughout this book we have discussed how this journey is yours to own. That means owning it until the very end.

Most of the goodbye content in this chapter is about when both you and your therapist have decided to end therapy, having determined that it has succeeded. But there are times when one-sided goodbyes happen. Maybe you realize that you need a different therapist, your therapist left the business, your therapist passes away, or you just aren't feeling it anymore. Not all goodbyes can be controlled, but say goodbye if you can. Goodbyes offer closure.

The process of getting closure means that you are finalizing the relationship or situation and moving on. With closure there is an understanding of why you went to therapy and why it's ending. Closure can also be healing. When something happens to us, we create a narrative around the event. It plays a part in how we view ourselves and the world. Without closure, we are left to make our own assumptions, which can skew our narrative around the situation. If you can have closure with your therapy process, I encourage you to take advantage of it. By getting closure, you'll be able to process what worked well and what didn't.

IT'S IMPORTANT TO SAY GOODBYE

You may know you are done before your therapist does. Hear me out: no longer wanting to go to therapy may be a sign that you are done. If you find yourself dreading the appointment or rescheduling, listen to yourself. Pause, and reflect on what is going on. Maybe therapy has been deprioritized, which is okay. Or maybe you feel that your therapist has taken you as far as you want to go.

I knew my therapy journey was coming to a close when I didn't have much to talk about during sessions. I also started to feel like the therapy appointments were interfering with my time, which I didn't feel before. When my therapist canceled a session because she was moving, I felt relief. It felt like I had gained an hour back. I realized, "Shit, we've come to the end." When my therapist asked to reschedule the canceled appointment, I really didn't want to. But I did, because I didn't want to leave without a proper goodbye.

During the last session, I talked about how good things were, my decreased flashbacks from my dog passing, and overall improved joy in my life. I felt guilty for wanting to stop abruptly, like I was going to be impacting her. My therapist sensed that something was different. When we had about 20 minutes left, she paused and said, "Shani, everything seems to be going well, and it's been two months since our last session. Why are you here today?" Holy shit, I felt called out. I was afraid to tell her I felt like I was done. She had taken me through grieving the loss of my dog and finding myself in my career. How could I just leave her?

My therapist went on to tell me that she felt I was ready to end. I knew it, but hearing her say it felt too real. We then discussed if I would schedule another appointment. I wasn't quite sure I was ready to say goodbye. I said, "Can we check in after two months by email to see if I need another appointment?" I knew I didn't need her anymore, and that reality was scary, so I wanted a safety appointment in place. It was scary because it meant acknowledging that I was growing and healing. It meant leaving the Shani who came to therapy behind.

Acknowledging my growth was scary. Sometimes, when I am experiencing situations, my awareness is so keen that I viscerally feel myself pause. I find myself asking, "How do I want to approach this situation?" This was scary for me because being unaware allowed me to have excuses for my previous behaviors; it let me place the blame elsewhere. Now that I have grown, I have to take accountability for my actions.

Then there is leaving the Shani who came to therapy behind. She is so special to me. I look back at her and see someone who had just lost a piece of her support system that showed her unconditional love, my dog Caspian. I had never experienced that type of love prior to getting him. I bought him after I graduated from undergrad. It was a very dark time in my life. My suicidal thoughts were constant, my drinking led to many nights of promiscuity, and seeing his cockapoo face at the end of the day made it all fade away. He was with me when I met my husband, moved to Minnesota, had our first kid, bought our first house, had our second kid, and moved to Arizona. I remember looking at him as he lay in my arms before giving him the second dose of euthanasia medication. I had leaned in and whispered, "I'm going to be okay, you're a good boy."

The veterinarian had emphasized the importance of saying goodbye to my dog and how it could benefit me. I believed those same benefits can be applied to saying goodbye in therapy. Going to the last session and saying goodbye to my therapist benefited me because I was able to put words to how I was feeling. This allowed me to label and identify what I was going through. Having had a positive and healthy memory around saying goodbye in the last session helped with how I remember our time together. A positive memory of a healthy goodbye was important to my growth. I don't have many moments in my past to help me model positive goodbyes. Instead of avoiding it, I faced the loss head-on and am now more confident that I can handle goodbyes, whether positive or negative.

Therapy has helped you feel better, and now you can navigate the work in an effective and authentic way. You're saying goodbye because therapy was effective. This is what makes the ending good. You have improved, healed, grown, and are going on to thrive. You probably have greater self-acceptance, self-knowledge, and self-awareness, all of which can positively impact the quality of your relationships. Now is the time to use those new skills to say goodbye. You've made it this far, and all that hard work you've done is deserving of closure.

HOW TO PREPARE FOR THE LAST SESSION

This will be the last time you meet with your therapist, the person who has been rooting for you since they first met you. There is no right or wrong way to "have" the last session, but there are ways to prepare for it.

DOPE EXPERT: JOHN JANKORD MA, LMFT, LADC, LPCC

John was my supervisor when I was training to be a therapist. His authentic and empathetic approach to the therapeutic relationship has left a lasting impression on how I show up as a therapist. Because of that, I asked him about preparing for the last session, and here is what he has to say.

> **How can a client prepare for the last session and saying goodbye to their therapist?**

As a therapist, I am preparing for the last session during the very first session. The client and I have no "formal" closing or last session planned, as our work is open to reconnecting in the future as needed. I invite the client to share what they are taking with them and reflect on what they learned about themselves.

Saying goodbye to your therapist is hard AF. How can someone best cope with the feelings that come up after they say goodbye to their therapist?

Similar to other endings (death, divorce, moving, etc.), I invite them to think about what they would like to hang on to and carry with them in the future, reinforcing the work, insights, and development they experienced while working together. It's more about remembering rather than getting over or saying goodbye.

I don't think clients know just how much they impact us as therapists. What do you think therapists wish their clients knew about saying goodbye?

I hope clients not only experience the care and appreciation during our working together but also carry those experiences with them as resources in the future. I want them to experience how important they are and how I've been influenced by and appreciate our work together.

~~~~~~

Ask yourself: "Are there any final thoughts that I would like to share with my therapist?" I recommend asking yourself this question a month before, a week before, and then the day before your last session. This will be the last opportunity for you to process with your therapist.

Lastly, create a maintenance plan with your therapist. Relapse occurs, and having a plan will be helpful. This plan is established to aid your success upon the completion of therapy. With your therapist you should 1) identify the primary reason you came to therapy, 2) identify the triggers and warnings, 3) identify ways to handle the triggers and warnings through self-care and coping skills, and 4) establish how you will know when it's time to return to therapy.

(This may be a great opportunity to return to Chapter 7 to reference self-care and coping skills.)

Muranda is feeling confident about ending therapy. She feels that she hit the goals she intended to reach. She came to therapy to learn conflict resolution skills with her husband but ended up learning how her parents' divorce impacted her thoughts about marriage. In the process, she also learned that she has an anxious attachment style, and when she feels distant from her husband, she uses activating strategies to seek intimacy. This is usually where the conflict comes from because her husband has an avoidant attachment style. So, when Muranda uses activating strategies, he uses deactivating strategies. Learning about her attachment helped her marriage as well as her relationship with family and friends.

Muranda and her therapist discuss the skills she will continue to use. Having weekly check-ins with her husband helps them see what worked during the week, what didn't work, and what they need to focus on in the upcoming week. In the past, Muranda felt that her husband's irritability would affect her own mood. She plans to continue working on not taking his mood personally. She does this by acknowledging that her husband is in a different mood than her, practicing a grounding technique to keep herself present and out of her thoughts, and then using an affirmation. To continue working on communication, Muranda and her husband plan to continue to use "I" statements and look at problems from an "us against the problem" perspective.

During the last session, Muranda and her therapist create a maintenance plan. Muranda started therapy because she and her husband were constantly arguing, which exacerbated her irritability related to her depression. She wanted to improve communication in her marriage and manage her feelings of being overwhelmed. A trigger for her was when her husband would leave mid-argument when she was asking for her needs to be met. She also realized that lack of sleep increased her feeling of being overwhelmed. Muranda and her therapist identify warning signs that Muranda can watch out for, such as her husband starting to ignore her needs and wants, Muranda feeling frustrated with the kids at bedtime, and her thoughts starting to race prior to bed.

In her therapy sessions, Muranda identified that she didn't get enough alone time, which can lead to increased overwhelm. With her therapist's encouragement, Muranda started spending one hour each week alone doing something she enjoyed. This gave Muranda something to look forward to, even if she had a busy schedule. She will continue doing this after ending therapy.

When it comes to arguing with her husband, once her husband's voice starts to fluctuate, Muranda can implement a boundary by telling him that she doesn't like the way he is talking, wait to see if he changes his voice, and if he doesn't, she can walk away. If Muranda recognizes that her thoughts are racing prior to bed, she now mind-dumps into her journal and then meditates.

The last thing on the maintenance plan is identifying how Muranda will know if it is time to return to therapy. They identify a few reasons for her to return to therapy: feeling overwhelmed three or more times a week, starting to think about divorce again, lacking the energy to put her kids to bed three or more times a week, or going two or more days without talking to her husband.

Muranda is looking forward to renewing her vows in the next year. She didn't realize how much doubt she had in her marriage and how her parents' divorce had played such a cancerous role in her thinking. She is now feeling optimistic about her marriage and often finds herself daydreaming about getting old with her husband, which she hadn't done before. In *addition, she finds she has increased energy to put the kids to bed and enjoy her alone time.*

THE LAST SESSION

You did it. You made it. You're about to have the last session with your therapist. The last therapy session isn't a pit stop; it's the inevitable completion of the journey.

You probably got a sense that therapy was coming to an end throughout the process. Or maybe you don't feel like it's time. Clients can sometimes resist the end of therapy. Although it should be discussed throughout, it doesn't necessarily lend itself to being easy. As it is a gradual process, your therapist will start to bring up the end before the last session. When this happens, notice how you are feeling and what thoughts you may be having. This will impact your behavior around the ending.

Yara is hesitant to go to her last session. She has been seeing her therapist for roughly two years. She is now moving to Portland and her therapist isn't licensed in Oregon. They agreed that Yara's next goal was to continue therapy with a new therapist once she moved to help cope with the transition. The previous session involved identifying what Yara needs from her new therapist. Yara had expressed that she felt like she will be starting over.

In the weeks leading up to the last session, Yara feels the urge to not show up. She struggles knowing that it will be the last time she'll see her therapist. She keeps thinking that there is no point to the last session, because nothing is going to be processed. She and her therapist have already established a plan. What else is left? Yara also doesn't want to say goodbye because she doesn't do well with goodbyes.

When Yara walks into the session, she immediately starts crying. In therapy she had learned to not flee from her emotions and instead vocalize them and sit with them. She mentioned several times that she doesn't like goodbyes because of her father. When she was younger, her father traveled a lot for work, never said goodbye, and made false promises for showing up to her events. This left her feeling anxious and abandoned.

"I think you're a good man, and possibly the best man in my life. Saying goodbye to you is like losing a father," she says to her therapist. "This is loss. Do you know what stage of grief you are in?" her therapist replies. "Sadness and anger," Yara states through tears. They spend the last minutes of therapy saying what they learned from each other. Yara leaves feeling closure and understanding the importance of saying goodbye.

Once the last session has started, you will discuss how you feel about ending therapy with your therapist. The increased insight that you have gained throughout the therapy process will help you clarify and identify how you feel about starting a new journey. It is okay to ask your therapist how they feel about the work you have done. The relationship doesn't end because you are ending therapy. Share with your therapist all the feelings and thoughts that you are having. If you have any questions, now is the time to ask.

Because success isn't a linear process, discussing what you learned about yourself will help you identify your growth. It is important for you to write down what you learned in your therapy journal. In the future, you may come across similar emotions, situations, and people, and being able to refer back to these lessons will help you after therapy ends. You'll also be able to identify how you healed through your lessons. Therapy creates resilience. Recognizing how you healed validates that resilience.

You'll talk about goals one last time. There should be a check-in around how you are feeling about hitting your goals. Being on the same page extends to the very last minute. You and your therapist will also come up with new goals now that therapy is done. What do you want to continue to work on? What areas do you feel require further guidance? What tools will you use to continue to work on these goals? And, of course, how will you sustain the goals that you met in therapy? That last stage of change may rear its ugly head without the guidance of your therapist, so talking about sustaining change is helpful.

Life doesn't stop because therapy stops. You will continue to face challenges, but you'll be more resilient and better equipped to handle them. You and your therapist can come up with a plan for challenges that you may face in the future. Name it so you can tame it.

Not needing your therapist is a good thing, but you may still want them. You may still want their input, their guidance, their empathy, and their company. These are normal feelings to have. Talking about how the therapeutic relationship affected you will improve your understanding of healthy relationships. Some relationships run their course in our lives, and holding on longer than needed can be more harmful than helpful. The relationship with your therapist may have been the first time in your life that a healthy interpersonal relationship was modeled and established. Although you do most of the talking about what you learned, it may be helpful to hear what your therapist learned from you. The impact of the relationship isn't one-sided. In this process, you can also offer your therapist feedback. Therapists are not allowed to ask for reviews as it is unethical, so offering your therapist feedback is a constructive way of identifying what was or wasn't helpful for you.

Before you walk out of the room or leave the video session for the last time, ask your therapist for resources. Resources for sustaining change, resources for ending therapy, and resources for continuing with your progress are beneficial. Discuss with your therapist how you are feeling and what you think about ending therapy. If you feel that you aren't ready, tell them.

Therapy is often a pivotal point in your life. It can shift you in a one-eighty, in a good way. I have encountered some clients who don't come to the last session and some that dip out of therapy right before the ending stage is about to start. It is normal to dread the end of therapy. The last session can mimic feelings of rejection. Although you know the end of the journey is near, you may not want it to end. However, having your therapist challenge this can feel like rejection. This is why being on the same page about the end of therapy is important. Communicating your feelings of rejection gives your therapist the opportunity to validate and process those feelings with you.

What if you feel triggered? We have all at one point or another had to say goodbye. What your past goodbyes look like can surface at the end of therapy. Ending therapy can take place over the course of several sessions in order to allow ample time to process and plan for the last session.

Or maybe you don't know how to say goodbye. There is no right way to say goodbye. Being in the moment with how you are feeling will let you know how you want to say goodbye. It's not always sad, just as it's not always happy. You may not process saying goodbye until after the last session.

DOPE EXERCISE: BEFORE THE LAST SESSION

Before your last session, think about the topics you want to address with your therapist. These might include the following:

- *What you were able to achieve in therapy*

- *What you didn't achieve in therapy*

- *The therapeutic relationship: what was helpful and what wasn't*

- *The feelings that saying goodbye is bringing up*

- *Any feedback you have for your therapist*
- *Your goals now that therapy is ending*
- *How to make an appointment if you want to return*

WHAT NOW?

You've said goodbye. You're entering the world as a changed person. I imagine there is something you took away from therapy that forever changed your thoughts, emotions, and behaviors. Now you can establish how you will continue to do the work. To do that, you need to identify what you will continue to work on. Think about the therapy journey: How did you heal? What changed? What worked? What didn't work? This will help you figure out the areas that you can continue to work on.

Did you know you can do check-ins, updates, or even come back? You may want to inquire with your therapist and ask them how they feel about updates. If you are someone who wants to send updates, know that you might not get a response, but that doesn't mean your therapist didn't see it. Depending on what is in the update, your therapist has to be conscious of how they respond as you are no longer a client.

> *Tu has been apprehensive about the last session with her therapist. She doesn't know how she would have found herself and defined her identity as a Vietnamese woman without the help of her therapist, having struggled with identity most of her life due to being adopted by white parents when she was four. She is also worried about the future, like what will happen if she is no longer able to manage her anxiety on her own.*
>
> *During her last therapy session, Tu asks her therapist about how she could go about making an appointment if she needs to. Her therapist explains that Tu can come back by emailing them and may have to fill out paperwork again, depending on how*

much time has passed. However, coming back is as easy as reopening her case. They also let Tu know that availability will depend on their schedule. Tu feels reassured and more confident that her therapist is available if she needs them. At the end of the session, Tu hands her therapist a bracelet. Making bracelets is one of Tu's coping skills for when she is having racing thoughts. Her therapist gladly accepts the bracelet.

When ending therapy, ask your therapist how they handle check-ins and follow-up sessions. Check-ins can be helpful if you are going through a transition or just want to check in to make sure things are still going well for you. You'll want to know the therapist's policy and how you can get on the schedule. Having a check-in session booked further out can feel more comfortable when easing out of therapy.

You'll also want to know what happens if you need to come back. How does this work with the therapist's schedule, and do you need to fill out paperwork again? Being prepared for how to return will help you if the time comes.

Keep in mind that you and your therapist are still not friends. Some people are tempted to move toward this direction, and now that you are no longer a client, you may feel compelled to reach out and try to be friends with your therapist. Some states require a certain amount of time to pass before your therapist can technically be your friend. However, it's usually not a good idea. The lines are still blurred. For one, it would be unbalanced. Your therapist knows way more about you than you do about them. And although you are not actively seeing them, they still were your therapist. If you become friends with your therapist, you won't be able to return as a client if you need to.

Gifts. Gifts are tricky as far as the therapist receiving them. Know that not all therapists are willing to receive gifts, and it could be an ethical violation. There are things that have to be taken into account, such as how much the gift cost, the client giving the gift, if giving a gift is cultural, and the ramifications of refusing the gift. If you want to give your therapist a gift and are unsure if they will receive it, ask. You can use the session prior to the last to talk about the gift that you would potentially like to give your therapist. If you want to give your therapist a gift, be aware that they may refuse it, but it's not you, it's them.

And that's it. If you are thinking about starting therapy, just starting, or in the thick of it, I am proud of you. You took the time to read a book to empower your journey and own it. In my eyes, that will not go unnoticed. Whatever life throws at you from here on out, remember therapy is always available to you. You're more resilient and insightful now that you know what to expect from the therapy process. The goodbye is the start to a new beginning because the work is never done. The end of the dope therapy journey is the start to a new and improved dope you.

DOPE TAKEAWAYS

» Saying goodbye to your therapist provides closure.

» Review your work in therapy.

» Ask your therapist about gifts if you want to give one.

» Prepare for the last session with questions you may have.

» Continue to do the work even after you end therapy.

CHAPTER
THIRTEEN

DOPE QUESTIONS

efore I head out and leave you to your dope therapy journey, I want to take the time to answer some questions that may not have had a place in previous chapters. I imagine you still have some questions, as one book cannot answer everything. So, I asked my wonderful community of supporters on social media to ask me questions that they have about therapy. If I couldn't find a place for them in the book, here is where they rest. I hope that this book will continue to be your resource to come back to throughout your journey.

Is it logical to go to therapy with an ex?

Here's the thing about therapy: it is for you. The first thing to identify is: "What is your Why for attending therapy?" Then identify what your ex has to do with your Why. Gaining clarity around the purpose that someone serves in your healing journey will increase your awareness of how you want your journey to go. As discussed in previous chapters, having people in your therapy sessions can be beneficial. It would also be helpful to bring it up with your therapist to gain further clarity and insight. Together, you and your therapist can come up with a therapy goal around having your ex join your sessions, if that is the direction you choose to go.

Do sessions with a client ever get to you—positively or negatively?

The answer is yes. As a therapist, I have been trained to recognize when my clients' stuff affects me. I don't want to say that it is positive or negative, just that it impacts me. I definitely have those moments when I walk out of a session feeling emotionally charged. Usually, I dance it off.

I'd like to consider myself a seasoned therapist because I don't bring my work home. I identify my home as my personal mental space. I don't let clients' stuff into my personal mental space where it could start to affect me as a person. This boundary is helpful and makes me a better therapist. If my clients' stuff were to affect me, the objectivity that I provide in the therapy room could be compromised. However, there have definitely been clients who have stuck with me after they ended services.

How do you know what to bring up in the first session?

The answer to this question applies to any session, not just the first. You can start wherever you would like. Even if your therapist starts the session off with, "How are you doing today?" feel free to answer with, "I'm doing blah blah blah, and here is what I would like to talk about . . ." This is also where your therapy journal will come in handy. If you're walking into a session and you feel like you don't have anything to talk about, it might be helpful to take a glance at your therapy journal. There's a lot that can happen between sessions, and having a journal will allow you to keep track.

And of course, let your therapist guide you. It is our job to keep you talking. Now with that, be mindful. If your therapist is guiding the sessions and you feel like you don't have anything to talk about, this could either be an interfering behavior, avoidance, an indication that your therapist is not a good fit for you, or a sign that therapy is coming to an end.

What are the misconceptions about therapy for people of color?

Y'all know I love talking about my people and my community. There are a lot of misconceptions about therapy for people of color. I want to answer the question from a Black person's perspective. It may pertain to people from other backgrounds as well, but because I am Black, I can only speak from a Black perspective. I do not want to speak for other communities and make assumptions.

In the Black community, I find that these misconceptions are often handed down from generation to generation. I grew up hearing and have often been told by other Black people that "we don't go to therapy" and "therapy isn't for us." Because the impact of these narratives can affect us through generations, we start believing these statements. To top it off, the mental health field is dominated by white people. I think it's always helpful to question the things that we have heard and analyze their factual integrity and origin.

If you have a certain perception of therapy, I want you to ask yourself: "Is that my perspective or someone else's?" If it is someone else's perspective, I encourage you to investigate therapy for yourself. If you have had an experience that has impacted how you think about therapy, check in with yourself to see if that experience is related to the therapist.

Negative experiences with therapy are usually rooted in the therapeutic relationship, whether that was the way the therapist did therapy, the connection between you and your therapist, or how you felt in therapy. Because of this, I encourage you to continue searching for a dope therapist. The right therapist can make a life-changing difference in how you experience therapy.

How do you know what kind of therapy you need?

Oh, this is a good one. There are different types of therapists, different types of modalities, and different areas of specialties. The different formats of therapy can be group, individual, family, couples, etc. The first thing is to identify who will be going to therapy. Will you be going alone, with a partner, or as a family? This will tell you if you are looking for an individual therapist, a couple's therapist, or a family therapist.

If you want to go to therapy with your partner and work on infidelity in the partnership, you may find it helpful to see a couple's therapist who specializes in working with couples who have experienced infidelity. If you want to go to therapy alone to feel more satisfaction when you are intimate, you may be looking for a therapist who specializes in sex therapy. When you contact therapists, ask them if they think their approach is the best one for you and your concerns.

When it comes to the type of modality, this one can be tricky to figure out on your own. Most people are familiar with Cognitive Behavioral Therapy (CBT), but there are so many other styles. The best way to know which modality works for you is to investigate how the therapist uses the different modalities to assist clients as they work through their concerns.

When do you know it's not working with your therapist?

Trust yourself and how you are feeling about the relationship with your therapist. Right now, I want you to identify how you feel about the therapist and why you feel that way. If you feel that it is not working with your therapist, you won't be able to benefit from therapy.

You also want to discern the difference between being stuck and not working. In therapy, being stuck is a feeling of not moving forward. Not working can be a little harder to identify because sometimes it gets worse before it gets better. It's not working if you start canceling sessions or don't feel like you're getting better. But remember to ask yourself: "Is it not working, or is this interference?"

No matter what your concern is, I encourage you to have a conversation with your therapist. By talking to your therapist, you can figure out if the issue is something your therapist is doing or something you are doing. You may want to revisit Chapter 10 to help you identify what's not working. Remember the therapeutic relationship is one of the indicators of the success of therapy. Take a step back and look at your goals and ask yourself: "Do I feel like I'm on track to meet my goals with my current therapist?"

How do you break it off when a therapist isn't the right one for you?

You can stop going. Literally, you can choose to stop going and not show up. I don't want to say that this is a negative thing. But, because the therapeutic process is about owning your journey, I want to encourage you to reach out to the therapist to let them know that you don't think it is a good fit.

The next way that you can break up with a therapist is through email. If you don't feel like you want to hear the therapist's input, email them and let that be that. I tried to break it off with my therapist at one point and, Imma be honest, the route I chose to take was email. But, being the amazing therapist that she is, my therapist decided to call me. And then, when I didn't pick up, she left me a voicemail. She suggested that we discuss it over a call, and that there would be no charge. During that process, I learned that she cared more about me than I thought she did. And, in talking to her about why I didn't think we were a good fit anymore, I realized what I was struggling with in the therapeutic relationship had been a misunderstanding. We talked it through and repaired it.

You can also bring it up in a session. There are many benefits to talking to your therapist when you want to end the relationship. You'll be able to explain why you want to end the relationship and have a conversation around what that looks like. Having a conversation with your therapist may give you a better understanding of what you need. Furthermore, therapists are ethically required to refer you, so you'll be able to get help finding another therapist.

There are some situations where harm is done in the therapy room. If you don't feel safe with your therapist anymore, or don't feel like you are in a space to let the therapist know, please feel comfortable to silently say deuces.

What happens to the notes y'all be taking?

Usually nothing. If you use insurance, your notes are accessible by the insurance company. If you don't use insurance, the notes are for you and your therapist. If your therapist has an office manager, they may be able to see the notes for billing and audit purposes. If your therapist is under supervision, their supervisor also has access to the notes. But for the most part, notes are a way to keep track of your progress. Now sometimes, but very rarely, a therapist's notes can be subpoenaed.

Did you know that you have access to your notes? That's right— you can ask for your notes. But recognize that you may not be ready to see what is in them. Although notes track their progress, sometimes clients aren't ready to read them. For instance, if a client talks about wanting to end an on-again, off-again relationship, my notes may state: "Client struggles to make a decision on whether they want to stay with their partner. Client presented as irritable and frustrated with making the decision." A client may not be ready to read that they are struggling, even if they know they are.

What is the hardest part of being a therapist for you?

I love the connection with people so much. I just freaking love people. I love helping people. I love watching people grow. I love the relationship part of therapy. I wish my clients could see themselves the way I see them. Sometimes I find myself wanting to self-disclose in a Tony Robbins motivational speech kinda way.

But I have to ask myself if what I'm about to say is going to be helpful to the client. And it's not always about the context of what I have to say. I'm a storyteller, so I love telling stories to inspire and motivate. I genuinely care for my clients and never want them to feel that our relationship is about me being "paid to care."

Watching people experiencing pain and feeling helpless is the toughest part. The journey of therapy ebbs and flows. Just like you may feel some therapy sessions work and some don't, as a therapist, I feel that too. And sometimes, I walk away from therapy sessions feeling like I wasn't helpful and sucked at my job that day. I can be hard on myself.

I have to hold back this desire to solve things for my clients. I don't like seeing people struggling. But I know that it is not helpful. Solving doesn't help. It may temporarily eliminate the struggle, but my clients don't learn anything from that. I remind myself that if I can model, teach, support, and validate, my clients will be more successful in life.

Will I be hospitalized if I say I am suicidal?

A client saying they feel suicidal is not enough to hospitalize them. The first thing a therapist should do is assess for severity. Is the client wishing to not be alive? Is the client thinking about dying by suicide? Does the client have a plan?

The therapist should also assess risk factors and protective factors (covered in Chapter 8) as they apply to suicide. A risk factor for someone with suicidal thoughts can be past attempts. A protective factor can be a strong support system.

Therapists must also assess for intent and planning. This means that if a client says they are suicidal, do they have a plan? The plan can be a time and a location. However, clients aren't always forthcoming with details, so there are other ways that a therapist can assess for a plan. Does the client talk as though the end is coming? Have they started giving things away? A plan can also show up in body language and connection. Sometimes people are calmer once they have made a plan, so a therapist may look for a sudden shift in mood. The therapist will also assess for intent or purpose; why does the client want to die by suicide?

There is no definite yes or no answer to whether a discussion of suicide will result in hospitalization, but talking to your therapist about how they handle hospitalizations may be a great way to build trust and help you feel open about discussing suicide with them.

How do I convince family and friends to go to therapy?

You can't. People have to be ready for the therapy process on their own. It is okay to have encouraging conversations around mental health and therapy. However, understanding the right time and place is important. The family Christmas dinner is probably not a good time. If you believe a friend or family member needs therapy, make sure that you have a strong enough relationship with them to approach the topic. Don't push for therapy during an argument or time of crisis when emotions are running high; bring up your concerns when they are in a good mood.

It may also be helpful to offer to go with them, help them find a therapist, or figure out their benefits. Sometimes the resistance to therapy is the work and energy it requires to start therapy. Remember that the purpose of the conversation is to encourage, educate, and empower, NOT to convince. Be prepared that there may be resistance and offer to help and support them, no matter what their decision is.

It may also be helpful to name their strengths during this time. When having the conversation with people around attending therapy, we as people have a habit of pointing out what is wrong. This is a great opportunity to voice positive things about your friend or family member.

Are there negative outcomes to pursuing therapy?

Well, that depends on how you look at it. There are side effects of going to therapy and one of them is change. When you change through therapy, it may feel like others around you are changing. For instance, you start implementing boundaries that upset people in your life. When you go to therapy and grow, you might realize that your current relationships aren't sustainable. Sometimes clients see this as a negative side effect. Losing people in your life was never the intention. But, as your insight and awareness grow, you become cognizant of the people that you keep in your inner circle.

Working with a therapist who works out of their scope of practice can also be a negative side effect and be harmful. For example, if you go to therapy to work on substance use but your therapist isn't trained in substance use, your therapist can harm you with their techniques.

Then there are therapists who struggle with boundaries. Unethical therapists often lack boundaries or attempt to infringe upon your own; they might make inappropriate comments, inappropriately touch you, stop doing their own therapy work, get triggered easily, or want to be your friend.

So, yes, therapy can be harmful. If you feel that you have had a harmful therapy experience, please don't hesitate to contact your state board and report the therapist. Therapy can be harmful when:

- Your therapist is unethical.
- Your therapist uses the wrong model or therapeutic technique.
- Your mental health gets worse, and you aren't forthcoming about it with the therapist.
- Your therapist lacks empathy.
- You experience side effects from medications that go unnoticed or are not communicated.

What do therapists do when you cry?

There is no general answer to this question; it depends on the therapist and their style. It also depends on your relationship with the therapist and the comfort and trust levels of your therapeutic relationship. Therapists are trained to handle cathartic moments. Overall, the therapist will be validating and supportive. If you are crying, it means that you are being vulnerable and are expressing something deep and meaningful. Our goal is to guide you through this cathartic moment in a safe and validating way. Then the therapist will help you identify and label your tears to help understand their cause. If the therapist is going to offer a hug or any sort of comfort through touching, they should always ask beforehand. When you cry, your therapist may be thinking:

- Is this a time to pause?
- How can this moment be used to gain insight and awareness?
- How can I help the client process what is happening right now?
- What does my client need right now?

How long should I be in therapy?

This can vary based on the type of therapy a client is receiving and the needs of the client. Some therapy modalities have a clear end time such as EMDR (Eye Movement Desensitization and Reprocessing). Therapy can be short, lasting only a few sessions. Or it can last for months or even years. There are many factors that come into play when understanding the duration of therapy. It is dependent upon your goals, your growth rate, the modality used, and costs. Some people may only come to therapy to address one specific issue. Some people may come to therapy with one issue but find that others surface. This is a great conversation to have with your therapist. For a better understanding of how long you can expect to be in therapy, checking in on your goals consistently will help you gauge where you are in the therapy process.

What happens if my therapist dies while we are working together?

Ahh, this one is a tough one because the person who is your support system passed away. Your therapist should have a plan in place to help their clients navigate what to do. In their plan, they should have someone who will contact their clients and specify what happens to your notes and how referrals are to be handled.

If you find yourself grieving, try to seek help from another therapist, specifically one who specializes in grief. They can help you identify what stage of grief you are in. Everyone grieves differently, and clarification on how you grieve will give more insight into what you need during this time.

How do I find a therapist who aligns with my political views?

When you are reading bios, pay attention to how you feel while reading. Look for that moment when you read a bio and you really hope that one therapist will call you back. Then, in the first session, explain to the therapist that political views are important for you and that you would like to ask them about theirs. Be mindful that not all therapists are forthcoming about themselves, and some may push back against answering personal questions.

Can you be a therapist if you've had mental health decline and have attended therapy in the past?

The answer is YES! When you apply for licensure, the application will include questions about your mental health, but it's not a hinderance to becoming licensed. However, be aware that not dealing with your own stuff can affect your clients. You can be in therapy while being a therapist. Everyone deals with stuff. If anything, that can make you a better therapist because you are able to truly feel empathy for your clients.

How is the length of a session decided?

A typical session is about 50 minutes if you self-pay and 53 minutes if you go through insurance. However, shorter and longer times are available. You'll want to talk to your therapist.

If your kid is in therapy, is it best to see the same therapist or your own?

This depends on your preference and the therapist. Some therapists prefer not to see individuals who are part of the same family. This is to give both you and your child your own therapy spaces. It also depends on whether you are in family therapy; sometimes you may see the therapist individually as part of that process.

When it comes to you, are you okay knowing that your therapist is also working with your child? I ask that because your therapist may be getting a different perspective from what you talk about in therapy, and this may inadvertently guide the questions they ask.

You may also want to ask the therapist how they approach working with members of the same family individually.

Do I have access to my teen's notes when they are seeing a therapist?

Absolutely NOT! Your teen going to therapy is for their benefit. In order to create a safe place for your teen, it is important that a safe harbor be established. The teen must know that what they talk to their therapist about will stay in the room. If a serious issue arises such as your teen planning suicide, this is a cause for their therapist to break confidentiality and inform you.

When I work with teen clients, I let the parents know that I would like them to be a part of the process, which means I ask them to send me updates on school and home. After establishing rapport with the teen, I let them know that I would eventually like to have their parents join. This is because the teen is still a part of the family system. And on the flip side, I let the parent know that I do not do drive-by counseling (i.e., this is not a situation where the parent drops the child off, assumes the child is the problem, and the parent never participates or gives updates).

How do I know if my relationship with my therapist is codependent?

To answer this question, let's start with what codependency is. Codependency incorporates your attachment style and refers to an unhealthy mental, emotional, or physical dependence on another person. In addition, people who struggle with codependency can need to feel needed. Your therapist does not need you. You need your therapist. You may be dependent on your therapist for guidance, mentally and emotionally, as that is what you came to therapy for. Being dependent on someone doesn't mean that you are codependent.

EXAMPLES OF CODEPENDENT BEHAVIORS

- You care what others think about you and measure your value against their opinion of you.
- You may struggle to accept praise.
- You belittle how you feel.
- You consider yourself selfless.
- You can be passive-aggressive.
- You may struggle when it comes to asking for your needs and wants to be met.
- You need others to feel safe.
- You struggle to set boundaries.

The first step is recognizing if you have codependent tendencies or have had codependent relationships in the past. Remember that therapy is a carbon copy of your life. There are things to look for in the therapeutic relationship that signal that you may be codependent. One sign is that you start changing to please your therapist. You may feel like your only choice is to make your therapist like you. This can show up when you start doing things for the benefit of getting your therapist to like you, such as homework. You'll notice this if you are doing and talking about things even if you don't want to, because your focus turns from you to the therapist. Crossing your therapist's boundaries is another sign. For instance if your therapist has told you they don't accept friend requests, but you keep trying. The stress of the therapeutic relationship could also be a sign, as seeing your therapist may become stressful because of how you think they view you.

I want to address that being dependent on your therapist is not a bad thing. You came to therapy because you need help. Therapy is an opportunity for you to learn how to be in a healthy relationship. Wanting and needing your therapist outside of sessions when you feel down, sad, or don't know what to do isn't codependent. If you feel you need another session, that's not codependent. It crosses the line into codependency when you start to care about what your therapist thinks and start changing your behavior to fit such a way, and it is unhealthy.

I hope I have armed you with knowledge and empowered you to seek your own dope therapy journey. Therapy requires communication for you to get the most out of the experience. If you feel uncomfortable with how therapy is going, communicate that. Your therapist can only guide you in the direction you want to go.

Don't forget to check in with yourself. Use your journal as a reference. You may not remember what your therapist says or does, but having a place for it all will help you when you're feeling stuck. And don't forget your Why. Let your Why guide you, motivate you, and comfort you. Now go out there and find yourself a dope therapist for your dope therapy journey. Deuces.

PS I'm proud of you!

ACKNOWLEDGMENTS

First and foremost, I want to say that I do not subscribe to the idea of the strong, independent Black woman. History has modeled that we keep our heads up, push through, and when they go low, we go high. But I absolutely refuse to subscribe to that. Sometimes when people go low, I go petty. Sometimes my vulnerability and tears are my strength. I refuse to wear myself out at the expense of a societal norm, no ma'am.

I have learned that it takes a village, and I need a support system to be able to do all the wonderful, creative work related to mental health that I do. It is okay for me to put my cape down because I refuse to pour from an empty cup.

My first shout-out goes to my wonderful, loving husband. This man is f*ck*n' amazing. He held down our home as a stay-at-home father while I built my therapy practice from the ground up, took on the social media space to become an influencer, went to school, and wrote a book. He made sure that when I got off work at 6 p.m., there was a hot meal with a vegetable waiting for me to scarf down. At night after working eight-plus hours and starting my homework, he would make sure I had a warm cup of tea. When I needed to rest on the weekends, he made sure the kids and dog didn't disturb me, essentially not having a day to sleep in himself. I don't know who said they don't need a man, but clearly, they haven't met mine!

To my two amazing, rambunctious, gregarious little girls: thank you for understanding that Mommy is doing big things! Thank you for the hugs and kisses at night that carried me through the long days.

Next, I want to say thank you to Michael from DK for seeing and believing in me. He approached me with the opportunity to write a book, and even when my original idea wasn't sh*t, he believed in me and told me to go back and try again. I honestly wouldn't have this publishing deal if it weren't for him. This white man saw this five-foot-two brown girl, thought she was the sh*t, and offered her a book deal. That doesn't happen every day!

Honestly, growing up I didn't have the best relationship with my mom, but today, she's my rock. Thank you for raising me. I know it wasn't easy being a single Black mother from the projects of Chicago. There were times when you thought you weren't capable of being my mother and I am sooooo glad you changed your mind. (You know what I'm referring to.) You raised me and helped me be the person that I am today. Thank you for always telling your friends to support me and buy whatever I am selling. Your belief in my abilities has helped me get to where I am today: a published author, business owner, and speaker.

I want to also give a shout-out to my father for always rooting for me and encouraging me to pursue becoming an author. I remember when I was in college and said I wanted to be a theater major and you just said, "Do it, Shani Girl." You have always supported my creativity.

Mama Tran, my husband's mother, you get a shout-out too. You have honestly changed the way that I view family and how I support my family. You helped us with the down payment of our first house, and that set me on a course to go harder and attain more so that one day I can help my children with their down payments too. It was this support that allowed us to focus on our careers instead of being financially stressed. For that, I am forever grateful.

I wouldn't be here if it wasn't for my TikTok supporters. Y'all vibe and f*ck wit me. I appreciate y'all so much. Because of your constant support, I was able to go viral and be seen. Because of your support, I became an influencer. Your comments on the videos that I post inspire me to keep going, and out of that, this book was born. I hope this book is an extension of what you see on TikTok, and you continue to be a part of this community.

To Berna, my bish! I didn't know that I could find a friend in this world who gives as much as I give. I've always longed for a brown girlfriend who loves traveling as much as I do. And then when I found out we had a book deal together . . . it was on. Thank you for listening to me rant and be explicitly vulnerable about the book writing process. Because of your support, I feel my writing days had a little extra spark. And thanks for the suggestion to listen to Harry Potter–inspired ASMR rooms while I write! I love you and can't wait to twerk with you again.

To all the Dope Experts who gave their time to answering my questions, thank you. All of you have things going on in your professional and personal lives, and I appreciate you taking the time to be a part of this book.

To all the people who didn't love me, you taught me great lessons about myself and who I am. I am thankful for the adversity you provided me to push through. You not loving me helped me lean into loving myself more. The pain that you created humbled me to the human experience, which has helped me be more empathetic as a therapist. You helped create this Shani, and for that I am grateful. Because the Shani I am today is a bad bish doing big things.

And last but definitely not least, thank you to the person who rejected me for the mental health job roughly six years ago. You said to me, and I will never forget, "You are meant for bigger rooms, and because of that, I cannot give you this job." That changed my life. From that moment, I started to really pursue the social media space, an outlet for my creativity. I knew I had to get myself in those bigger rooms. I am proud to let you know I am in those rooms. Thank you for seeing me.

I did it. I wrote a book with the help of my support team. To every human who has believed in me and my abilities, ***fist pump***

INDEX

C

cancellations. *See* no-shows and cancellations

Carnes, Patrick, 169

Casey, Kristen, 13, 157–159

CBT. *See* Cognitive Behavioral Therapy

Client-Centered Therapy, 89

closure, 237–251

check-ins, 250

continuing your work post-therapy, 249–251

feeling triggered, 248

importance of saying goodbye, 238–241

indication of therapy journey ending, 239

Jankord, John (preparation for last session), 241–242

last session, 245–249

exercise before, 248–249

preparation for, 241–245

maintenance plan, 242

Muranda's story, 243–245

resources, asking for, 247

takeaways, 251

Tu's story, 249–250

Yara's story, 245–246

codependency, 266–267

Cognitive Behavioral Therapy (CBT), 65, 89, 257

Colier, Nancy, 183

collective trauma, 177

complex trauma, 179

coping skills

development of, 208

examples of, 208–209

figuring out your, 208

maladaptive, 24, 31, 209

countertransference, 104

crying, therapist response to, 262

cultural competency, 72–73

cultural humility, 72–73, 172

D

Dawn Health, 159

DBT. *See* Dialectical Behavioral Therapy

defense mechanisms, 210–211

denial, 210

displacement, 210

projection, 210

rationalization, 210

reaction formation, 211

regression, 210

repression, 210

sublimation, 211

denial, 210

Desta, Dr. (knowledge on trauma), 168–169

m

n

o

SHANI TRAN is a Licensed Professional Clinical Counselor and the creator of The Shani Project and its associated TikTok channel, which offer insight into the world of therapy. She has been featured in the *New York Times*, *USA Today*, *Teen Vogue*, and *Cosmopolitan*. Her focus is on education around cultural humility and working with people of color. Dancing, all-inclusive vacations, and spending time with her family while eating food are a few of her healthy coping skills.